Khalilah Olokunola

Do Recruit

How to find and keep great people.

To my late Mom, Marietta, and Dad, David, who passed away before I could finish. To the HR pros who use their seat at the table for impactful change. And to those who have been overlooked in the hiring process. I hope *Do Recruit* shines a light on you.

Published by
The Do Book Company 2024
Works in Progress Publishing Ltd
thedobook.co

Text © Khalilah Olokunola 2024
Illustration © Hannah Cousins 2024
Author portrait © Peter Castagnetti
2022

To find out more about our company, books and authors, please visit **thedobook.co** or follow us **@dobookco**

5 per cent of our proceeds from the sale of this book is given to The DO Lectures to help it achieve its aim of making positive change: **thedolectures.com**

Cover designed by James Victore
Book designed and set by Ratiotype
Printed and bound by OZGraf Print
on Munken, an FSC® certified paper

MIX
Paper from
responsible sources
FSC® C163799

A CIP catalogue record for this book is available from the British Library

ISBN 978-1-914168-30-7

10 9 8 7 6 5 4 3 2 1

Contents

Prologue

My story begins with Dr. Seuss.

We all have 'Aha' moments in life that forever change us. It can be something as simple as a chance encounter, or it could be an epiphany that alters the course of our life. Well, mine came in the form of a series of children's books. I had decided to close my events business to pursue something more meaningful. Little did I know this path would take me on an incredible journey and change my life, for the better.

I had been wanting to do something more purposeful with my career — something that would empower women — but I wasn't sure what exactly. Then, one day, I had an idea: what if I used some of my favourite Dr. Seuss books to help people reach their full potential?

It seemed unconventional, but I decided to try it.

I realised that Dr. Seuss books were not only classics, they offered valuable leadership lessons that could be applied to so many real-life situations.

The Lorax teaches us the importance of being an advocate for those without a voice. The book focuses on the environment and taking action to protect it. The Lorax speaks for the trees and shows us that it's important to take a stand for what we believe in, even when it's difficult.

Horton Hears a Who! is a lesson in empathy and inclusivity. Horton teaches us to value every voice and every individual, no matter how small or different they may seem. He shows us the importance of listening and being there for others, even when it's challenging.

Oh, the Places You'll Go! is all about perseverance and the journey of life. It encourages us to take risks, face challenges and keep going even when things get tough. It reminds us that we have the power to shape our own destiny and achieve great things if we stay determined and resilient.

Green Eggs and Ham is a lesson in persuasion and the power of a positive attitude. Sam-I-Am never gives up persuading a man to try green eggs and ham. Eventually the man is convinced, and ends up loving it.

These, and many other Dr. Seuss books, offered valuable lessons in leadership, empathy, perseverance and positivity at a time of transition for me. By applying these lessons in my own life, I was able to become a better leader and make a positive impact on the community I served. It also helped shape my perspective on how I viewed people, places and things.

Could the books have a similar impact on others, I wondered? There was only one way to find out. I developed a course and began marketing it.

Of course, only one person came to the first session! But that soon became three, and three became 50 — all interested in taking part in my programme. Gradually, it caught the eye of others and I was booked for a speaking engagement at an event in New York City. This was where I met George Taylor from Wilmington, a small coastal town in North Carolina.

After the event, we had a conversation that would change everything. He shared his vision to create a brewery in his hometown that would hire active gang members. George had witnessed a drive-by shooting in his neighbourhood and wanted to take action. The brewery would be a social enterprise with a clear mission to unite and create understanding between rival gangs in order to better the community. In truth, I thought he had lost his mind.

Growing up in Brooklyn, New York, I was all too familiar with the lifestyle of gangs and their members. But when George opened his heart, I decided to share a personal story from my past as evidence that opportunity can truly change someone's life.

He invited me to share that same story with his team. That led to a 40-day contract and the beginning of what became the organisation's onboarding programme — and for me, a decade as Chief People Officer for TRU Colors Brewery.

Working with gang members made me realise how important it is for companies to focus not just on what candidates can do or have done, but also on who they are as people. I saw first-hand how so much of what we learn through life experiences can be used in corporate settings if we're given the right opportunity and the necessary support.

I remember one individual in particular. During the interview, he quickly impressed us with his enthusiasm for learning new things and dedication to improving himself each day. Despite his lack of traditional qualifications, we took a chance on him — and it paid off tenfold. After completing our onboarding programme and gaining valuable experience with our team, he went on to obtain higher-education credentials. Today he's running his own successful business venture.

My journey started with Dr. Seuss and that led me to TRU Colors. As the person responsible for hiring and retention, I had to find ways to create an inclusive workplace culture, build trust and, in the run-up to the closure of the brewery, navigate the team through a particularly challenging year. We faced a multitude of hurdles — from money struggles to management issues, and external factors like media scrutiny that further compounded our problems. We also experienced the painful loss of two team members.

As my time at TRU Colors came to an end, I was invited to lead a session on Living Empathy for a DO Lectures workshop called Bonfire with Soul, hosted by Duke Stump. 'Living Empathy' was something I applied at home and in the workplace. This reshaped perspective changed the narrative of everything I did, everything I built and everything I used for the people I have had the honour of serving. Today I consider myself an Impact Architect. I only build that which brings impact.

So, as we begin our journey into hiring and retention, I want you to understand that every word, every tool, every technique and every story shared is a product of my personal journey. I've walked this path and have tested these concepts in the real world, often facing trials and making errors. I've failed more times than I've succeeded, but it's those failures and lessons that have brought me to this point.

Recruitment, for me, isn't just a mechanical process. It's an invitation to build community. It's about welcoming individuals into a space where they feel a sense of belonging and can contribute to the wider company. It's a profound responsibility, a shared journey where, together, we craft a culture we can genuinely take pride in. Let's get started.

Introduction

In the ever-evolving world of talent acquisition, founders, business leaders and HR professionals are facing a unique challenge. The global pandemic of 2020, the resulting Great Resignation and job market crises have highlighted the need for creative thinking in the realm of talent recruitment and retention.

In recent years, we have seen employees favouring work-life balance, greater flexibility and the culture of a company over mere financial compensation. They are putting greater emphasis on the alignment of personal values with their workplace. We are also seeing the retirement of the baby boomer generation, leaving a significant talent gap in the workforce. And more of us are bravely venturing into entrepreneurship and creating companies of our own.

Lived experiences are learning experiences that can be used to lead others, and mine have taught me invaluable lessons. Chiefly, that life skills can translate into boardroom scenarios, given the chance. My journey in human resources that favours fair or second-chance hiring, particularly at TRU Colors, required assessing candidates through a unique lens. We placed significant emphasis on personality traits and character qualities, such as resilience and loyalty. We celebrated soft skills and implemented strategies to teach the necessary hard skills. This approach established trust with prospective employees from the start.

It's about looking beyond what a candidate can do or has done, and focusing on who they are as individuals. I call it 'whole person' recruitment. This is vital because the commercial world evolves in response to global events, and we need adaptable individuals who can pivot and perform under changing market conditions.

My hope is that this book becomes your trusted guide when navigating this ever-evolving recruitment landscape. I've placed an emphasis on mission, vision and values, as I firmly believe that our businesses and organisations can, and should, be centred around people, driven by a meaningful purpose and aligned with profitability.

I will equip you with the tools, techniques and knowledge needed to reshape your recruitment practices, centring them around responsible and ethical HR. The goal is to make your company an attractive choice for today's pool of job seekers. I hope every reader is inspired to revolutionise their hiring strategy to emphasise inclusivity, data-driven decision-making, ethical responsibility and innovation.

When it comes to recruiting, it's crucial to think differently and look beyond mere qualifications. While skills and experience are important, hiring isn't about creating duplicates of existing team members. Instead, it's about bringing in individuals who can enhance your collective efforts. The heart of innovation lies in the inclusion of people with different life experiences and perspectives, which enables the organisation to adapt and restructure its offerings to drive revenue. This approach benefits both the company and its employees.

The ultimate goal of any recruitment process is to find the right people for the right roles. By employing effective recruitment strategies, you can create a fair and equitable plan for all applicants. These strategies go beyond traditional approaches, accepting and embracing candidates for who they are, with their unique experiences, aspirations and dreams.

This ensures that talented individuals are matched with opportunities based on their true potential, rather than predefined identities. Such alignment can lead to profound transformations beyond the hiring room, advancing the world exponentially. Recruiting with intention sets your business up for success, as people begin to watch not just what you do but how you bring individuals in, how you treat them and how you navigate the process as and when they leave. I am thrilled to share the concept of responsible recruiting with you.

Be unconventional. Set true talent free.

Part one
Recruitment

1
Hire the whole person

When recruiting, it's not just about finding someone with the right skills and experience, it's about finding someone who will add value to your team and to your organisation.

This is why 'whole person' recruiting has become a popular approach in recent years. By taking a holistic view of potential applicants, recruiters can find the right combination of talent, skills (soft and hard) and character. We need people in place who can pivot if there is a problem, can take the baton when necessary and understand that the workplace is not just where you earn, but also where you learn.

The Full Person framework

When I'm recruiting, I think about: **Head, Heart, Hand and How**.

Together, these four aspects form the basis of my Full Person framework — a comprehensive, holistic framework for assessing individuals and making informed hiring decisions. The concept was based on my own experience taking the industry-standard Predictive Index assessments, which led me to the importance of evaluating behavioural drives, cognitive abilities and motivating factors. I call these 'Momentum Triggers' — factors that activate individuals to do their work with strength, drive and passion. It's an approach that unlocks human potential as it provides a better understanding of someone's full capability and likely contributions to the organisation.

By considering all four factors — Head, Heart, Hand and How — employers can ensure that they are hiring candidates who possess not only the necessary skills and qualifications, but also the right attributes for the job and values that align with the company's culture and mission.

The Head

Let's start from the top. 'The Head' refers to a candidate's cognitive abilities and emotional intelligence. Reasoning, problem-solving, abstract thinking and learning from experience are all mental capacities that fall under cognitive ability. It's what allows us to tackle challenges and handle pressure in a fast-paced environment. And in today's workplace, you need to ensure that the person you're hiring can pivot and adapt when there's a problem.

As you assess a candidate's cognitive ability to perform the job, ask yourself: Does their attitude and mindset align with the demands of the role and the potential for disruption within the industry... and the wider world?

In the wake of unprecedented global events like the Covid pandemic and the societal shift following the death of George Floyd in 2020, we found ourselves collectively navigating uncharted territory. The workplace challenges that emerged during this time were multi-faceted, from the need to adapt to remote working to the significant loss of staff following the Great Resignation — including employees who left companies that didn't take a stand or improve their Diversity, Equity & Inclusion (DE&I) initiatives, among many other reasons.

We all, in one way or another, became witnesses to these extraordinary events. Many of us were confronted with redundancy and job insecurity, while others were tasked with difficult decisions about making reductions in the workforce. We saw traumatic events on the news and experienced them in our personal lives. In the context of the Head, it was becoming clear that having the right mindset had become an indispensable asset.

Let me share a brief anecdote from my previous job. When the United States went into lockdown, just like everyone else, we had to adapt to a new way of working. However, what set our organisation (TRU Colors) apart was our ongoing commitment to ensure continuous employment for our staff to keep them engaged and prevent the escalation of violence. Our work remained not only necessary but critical. We were a brewery, but the actual product we were making was peace. To this day, I'm overwhelmed by the collective mindset of resilience, determination and optimism I experienced there. It enabled us to weather the storm and chart a course. This part of the Full Person framework in recruitment is so vital.

There is a power in having the right mindset. In times of uncertainty, the perspective it gives truly matters. It's about not surrendering to challenges or succumbing to adversity; it's about possessing the ability to push forward when everything seems to be urging you to concede defeat. The Head component will help you to identify individuals who won't simply raise the white flag when faced with adversity.

During interviews, put forward work-related scenarios that will help you to gauge the candidate's reactions and reveal their cognitive capabilities to adapt, think critically and engage effectively. This could be a made-up scenario or something that actually happened within the business. You will gain insights into whether they possess the mental dexterity to thrive in the position. A candidate may have an impressive resume and substantial technical skills but if their cognitive approach doesn't align with the demands of the role, it could lead to inefficiencies and conflict.

Take a moment to reflect: do you need to recruit someone who has experience of dealing with change? Have your sales been on a downward trend and do you need a more innovative approach? Are you currently facing a situation that demands a specific mindset? These are questions to ask yourself as you consider whole person recruitment.

The Heart

'The Heart', appropriately enough, is about getting to the heart of the matter. It seeks to unveil what truly fuels a candidate's enthusiasm and commitment. By understanding their core motivators, you can better gauge whether they naturally align with the company's mission and values, and can benefit the culture of your organisation.

While we talk about the interview in Chapter 5, two powerful questions to ask that unlock insights into the Heart are:

— **Tell me about yourself:** This question goes beyond the standard request for a candidate's background and experience. It invites them to share their personal or professional journey, emphasising what they consider

to be defining moments and accomplishments.
By narrating their own story, they reveal not only a
bit about themselves but also their career trajectory
and the values they hold dear.

— **Tell me a moment you're most proud of:** This question
will reveal the candidate's professional achievements.
Their response provides a window into what they
truly value and where they derive their sense of
accomplishment. This moment of pride often reflects
their core motivations, their capacity for problem-
solving and their ability to thrive under challenging
circumstances, which is also connected to the Head
and the How.

Understanding a candidate's passions and source of pride
is invaluable. By gaining a clear picture of what truly drives
them, you can make a more informed decision about their
fit within your team and their potential for contributing to
your company's wider mission. The Heart is about ensuring
that your new hires are not just skilled and experienced,
but also connected to the heartbeat of your company.

The Hand

'The Hand' refers to a candidate's knowledge, technical
skills and experience. It's what they can do. If a candidate
lacks the skills needed to perform the duties of the job
effectively, you have the option of providing them with
a professional development plan (we'll come to this in
Chapter 7) to bridge any gaps. Sometimes a candidate's
intangible qualities outweigh their practical skills so it's
important to consider that while knowledge can be gained

and technical skills can be taught, some things, such as character, cannot. This brings us to a key question that companies must ask themselves:

Are you open to candidates who may not possess the complete skill set? In other words, are you willing to invest in training to bridge the gap, or would you rather go with a candidate who already has all the technical skills and experience required?

The traditional approach to recruitment often emphasises hiring individuals with extensive experience and a comprehensive skill set. However, in the evolving employment landscape, where adaptability and a growth mindset are highly prized, this approach might need to be more relaxed for certain roles.

I should stress that when discussing Hand skills in these instances, I'm talking about roles where the skills needed can be acquired in a reasonable time frame through training — either in-house or externally. A doctor, for example, will always need to have the technical skills and expertise required to do their job!

So, the question here is whether you are willing to consider candidates who are eager to invest in their own professional development. This approach acknowledges the *potential* of individuals who, despite not meeting all prerequisites at the outset, have the determination and capacity to learn and grow. We'll get into how you can assess whether candidates have that capability in the Interview chapter.

Essentially, the Hand encourages a shift from a rigid focus on experience to a more flexible and forward-thinking perspective that values potential and adaptability. This new approach can open the door to a wider pool of candidates. It recognises that skills can be acquired and developed over time, often leading to more well-rounded and dedicated team members. It's an approach that has been key for companies that have adopted fair or second-chance hiring policies. In other words, they are willing to hire the right person for the job regardless of their background or obstacles preventing them from finding meaningful work.

It's a paradigm shift that recognises that the most valuable candidates are those who are not only competent but show a willingness to evolve and contribute to the organisation's future growth. It reflects the changing dynamics of the job market, where agility and a commitment to learning are vital.

The How

Lastly, 'The How' examines a candidate's adaptability and resilience. Have they encountered challenging circumstances that required them to pivot, shift or adapt to achieve their goals? Have they navigated high levels of staff turnover or managed change effectively? If so, *how did they do it?*

Both adaptability and resilience are crucial traits in today's dynamic work environment. You're probably wondering how the Head and the How differentiate. I know they seem similar, but they're quite different.

The Head assesses a candidate's cognitive ability: their problem-solving skills, critical thinking and intellectual capacity. It also examines their attitude and mindset, determining whether their mental outlook aligns with the demands of the role. This part of the model concerns their intellectual and emotional readiness to perform the job effectively.

The How is about a candidate's adaptability and resilience. It explores whether they've encountered challenging circumstances that demanded them to pivot, shift or adapt to reach their goals. And if so, what did they do? What was the outcome? So, this part of the model is about their practical experiences navigating change, managing adversity and handling unexpected challenges.

Ok, back to the How. We often face unexpected challenges at work that demand quick thinking and resourcefulness. For instance, you might have to deal with sudden market shifts or customer preferences.

Organisational change within a company, including mergers or restructurings, can create turbulence. Individuals who have successfully navigated through these periods of change demonstrate not only their professional acumen but also their emotional intelligence. How they maintained productivity during such periods would highlight their ability to focus or their leadership skills, for example.

Change is inevitable in any company. How candidates manage change, whether it's implementing new technologies, restructuring workflows or introducing new processes, reflects their problem-solving abilities and tenacity. And those who can guide their teams or teammates through change while maintaining a positive environment possess a rare skill set. More than just technical competencies, this reveals deep insights into their character. Resilient individuals approach challenges not as insurmountable obstacles but as opportunities to learn and grow. This makes them invaluable to any business aiming for sustained growth and success.

By using this 'Head, Heart, Hand and How' model, you can define the criteria for your ideal candidate, making it conducive to fair and second-chance hiring. As we've discussed, this approach revolves around selecting the best person for the job without allowing background, disability or any circumstances that others might label as barriers to hinder the process. It's an approach that naturally promotes inclusivity and diversity.

Adopting this model empowers you to look beyond conventional criteria and consider the unique experiences and diverse backgrounds that candidates bring. Interviews will be conducted with a better understanding of what you're seeking, which in turn will enhance the efficiency of the recruitment process.

By hiring candidates who possess all four qualities encompassed in the Full Person framework — the Head, Heart, Hand and How — you are building a workforce that is not only competent and productive but also motivated, emotionally intelligent and aligned with the company's mission and values. This, in turn, leads to higher job satisfaction, better employee retention rates and a more positive work environment.

2
The narrative

Welcome to the world of language in recruitment, where the four pillars of Foundation, Framework, Flow and Finish will serve as the building blocks of your discerning language strategy.

Language is crucial to a successful hiring process, whether that's in face-to-face conversations or how you phrase job descriptions. Crafting your narrative can create an irresistible draw for some because words affect emotions, which leads to a response. The right words can attract the perfect candidates for a job. But be cautious, as the wrong words could put off your ideal match.

For instance, job descriptions emphasising a fast-paced, highly interactive environment may discourage people who are more introverted. Job ads using complex technical jargon only understood by those 'in the know' could be intimidating and off-putting to others equally capable. Those that do not state 'equal opportunity employer' may lead people to think otherwise. So, choose your words wisely, as you want to bring people in, not drive them away.

The four pillars

All your written communications, whether that's a job description or an email to a new hire, should include what I call the four pillars: foundation, framework, flow, and finish.

The foundation is your objective and opening statement. Determine the primary purpose. Once you have that, start with an attention-grabbing opener that sets the tone. This could be a compelling anecdote, a surprising fact, a rhetorical question or a vivid description that piques the interest of a potential candidate.

The framework is the context you provide. Explain the background and relevant information so the candidates you are targeting have a clear grasp of the job description and the company that's hiring.

The flow is the logical sequence of the information you're sharing. For a job description, it's the title, duties and requirements. Make sure each part naturally leads to the next.

The finish is the close and an opportunity to make final checks and edits. Ensure that your tone of voice is consistent throughout. Conclude by summarising the main points and leave your audience with a clear understanding of, for example, what the job is and their next steps should they wish to apply. This is essential for written communication. Review and edit for clarity and coherence, eliminating any unnecessary details or information.

Subject: Digital Marketing Manager Opportunity

The foundation — opening hook:

Are you passionate about driving digital marketing strategies that make a real impact?

The framework — context:

At [Company Name], we're working to revolutionise how people experience [Product / Service]. As a growing tech start-up in the heart of [Location], we seek a dynamic and creative Digital Marketing Manager to join our team.

The flow — relevant information:

— *Briefly introduce the company and its mission.*

— *Describe the current marketing challenges or opportunities the company faces.*

— *Role: explain the key responsibilities of the role.*

— *Team: highlight the collaborative environment and the talented team the candidate will work with.*

— *Qualifications: list the qualifications and skills necessary for the job. Ensure that the list is clear, concise and free of any spelling, grammar or punctuation errors.*

— *Benefits: mention any benefits of joining the company, such as career growth opportunities or unusual perks.*

— *Provide clear instructions on how to apply.*

THE NARRATIVE

The finish — descriptive language:

In this role, you will have the chance to shape the digital marketing narrative of our brand, utilising cutting-edge tools and technologies to reach our target audience. You'll be working alongside a team of driven marketers who are as passionate about [Product / Service] as you are.

Engage emotionally:

We're not just looking for someone to fill a position, we're seeking a marketing maverick to fill a gap — someone who can share our vision and contribute to our exciting journey. Join us in making a difference in the lives of [Target Audience].

Closing:

Ready to be part of something big? If you're excited about making meaningful impact and driving the success of our digital marketing efforts, we'd love to hear from you. Apply now and help us write the next chapter of our story!

Subject:
Re: Your Application for Digital Marketing Manager

The foundation — opening hook:

> *Thank you for expressing interest in the Digital*
> *Marketing Manager role at [Company Name].*

The framework — context:

> *I hope this email finds you well. We were genuinely*
> *impressed with your application and wanted to*
> *share more about the exciting narrative we're*
> *building here at [Company Name].*

The flow — important points to include:

— *Acknowledgement: express gratitude for the*
  candidate's application.

— *The challenge: briefly touch on the marketing*
  challenges/opportunities.

— *Their role: describe the candidate's potential impact*
  in the role.

— *The team: mention the collaborative team atmosphere.*

— *Qualifications: highlight the candidate's qualifications.*

— *Next steps: invite the candidate for an interview or*
  further discussion.

THE NARRATIVE

The finish — descriptive asset-based (positive) language:

Your experience in [mention specific relevant experience] stood out to us. This is a key role in crafting our digital marketing story, using innovative tools and strategies to engage our audience, working alongside our passionate team, where creative ideas are encouraged and celebrated.

Engage emotionally:

We're not just looking for another team member; we're searching for a dynamic marketer who can become part of our story. Your skills and expertise appear to align with our vision.

Closing:

Are you ready to be part of our narrative? If so, we'd love to schedule a conversation to explore how you can contribute to our ongoing success. Please let us know your availability for a virtual interview. We look forward to connecting and learning more about your journey in marketing.

Incorporating narrative elements using the four pillars makes the job opportunity more engaging and allows you to describe the company's story and culture. The language you use will determine how you connect with candidates and, in turn, how they view your brand. And that's where a discerning language strategy comes in.

What is a discerning language strategy?

This is a thoughtful approach to communication that emphasises clarity, inclusivity and respect for diverse backgrounds. It involves selecting words that promote a positive, inclusive environment. Incorporated within the four pillars, it will align and strengthen your messaging. Key elements of this strategy are:

Asset-based language: By that I mean positive, inclusive communication. This is about using language that empowers all individuals regardless of their gender, race, age, religion or ability. In the Resources section at the back of the book, I've added a Word Bank with a list of asset-based words that can be used in interviews or conversations, as well as non-asset based words that should be avoided.

Clear communication: This ensures that messages are easy to understand and free from jargon or ambiguity, encouraging open and honest dialogue.

A considerate tone: This means maintaining respect and empathy, even in challenging exchanges.

Cultural sensitivity: This is challenging because none of us know everything, but being aware of cultural differences and avoiding language that may inadvertently offend or marginalise individuals from diverse backgrounds is vital. In the Resources section, I've added a Word Bank to help with this.

Values alignment: This aligns the language you use with your company's values and mission. It creates consistency in messaging and reinforces the company culture.
For example:

— **Environmental Responsibility:** if a company values environmental responsibility, they should use language that reflects their commitment to sustainability.
For example, they might say, 'We are dedicated to minimising our carbon footprint through eco-friendly practices' instead of 'We do our best to be green'.

— **Diversity and Inclusion:** a company that strongly emphasises diversity and inclusion might say, 'We are committed to shaping a workplace that embraces all backgrounds and perspectives' instead of 'We hire people from different backgrounds'.

If you're wondering how to seamlessly integrate this discerning language strategy and its key elements into your interview questions, we unlock that box in Chapter 5.

For now, just know that the correct language serves as the bridge that connects individuals to your organisation. It shapes your brand, builds relationships, attracts top talent and sets a welcoming tone. In recruitment, language isn't just words, it's a strategy.

3
Rethinking platforms

Let's face it, recruiting is tough. Finding the right candidate for the job can be a daunting task, especially with short timelines, limited resources and multiple stakeholders involved.

I've lived it and learned through it. Even some HR professionals prefer to avoid it, opting to work with recruitment consultants instead. The challenge lies in the many components required to bring in the right talent for the right position. And a critical component is where to place your listing or which platform to use. These platforms are the bridges that connect talent with opportunity, and in today's landscape you're going to need to find some alternative bridges.

From your company website to the professional look and feel of LinkedIn, to the edgier, tool-heavy vibe of Indeed and Monster, not only are there multiple platforms but each has its own personality. And when recruiting, it's essential to be aware of the distinctive personality of your chosen platform so you can tailor your listings accordingly.

In this chapter, we explore some of the platforms your future employees are likely to engage with when looking for new opportunities online. And how a better understanding of these platforms can help you shape your language and leverage tools to ensure your company and listings are presented at their best and in the ideal place.

I recall during a critical time for the brewery, things were going well overall but we faced some challenges, as any organisation does. After completing our latest eight-week onboarding with 12 rival gang members, we still needed to fill some key roles — positions that required certain knowledge and skills. Despite trying everything, the positions remained vacant. It was a tough period. The CEO (Chief Executive Officer) and COO (Chief Operating Officer) weren't too happy about it and all eyes were on us. It seemed like no one understood the difficulties we faced. There was a misconception that recruiting was easy but, especially at that time, that couldn't be further from the truth.

We posted on all the usual hiring platforms, but it wasn't working. Despite all the efforts of our team and HR director, our weekly meetings became a series of disappointments. It was at that moment that I knew we needed to change tack. I started looking more closely at the platforms on which we were recruiting, the methods we used and the language in our job descriptions to communicate who we are and why someone should join us. That was when I realised the crucial role that platforms play in finding the right people for a company.

You see, your method could be right, your strategy efficient, but you may not be getting any traction because of the platform you have posted the job vacancy on.

Think of the platform you recruit from as a lively hangout in your friendly neighbourhood, the spot where you find everyone you need. Just as people have their own preferred hangouts, online platforms cater to various needs and preferences. For example, many of us like LinkedIn for its multi-faceted offerings like community engagement and courses, as well as job opportunities. Others prefer Indeed for a more straightforward job search without the need for an extensive profile. Whereas others might favour more social platforms like Facebook.

We used various mainstream platforms like LinkedIn, Indeed, Glassdoor, ZipRecruiter, Workable and Monster, which offered both free and paid-for options. Here's a quick overview:

LinkedIn is the go-to platform for building your professional network, connecting with colleagues and industry peers, and showcasing your resume. Users come here to advance their careers, network and make industry connections. It's the leading platform for job seekers and employers alike. Users expect to find job postings, and companies use it for recruitment. LinkedIn provides valuable industry insights, thought leadership content and company news. Users here are also interested in staying informed and educated about their fields.

Monster is primarily job focused. Users come here explicitly for job searches and recruitment. It's known for its resume database, helping recruiters find candidates who may not even be actively job searching.

Indeed is a search engine designed to help people find jobs. It collects job postings from multiple sources and presents them in one place for easy access. Users visit to find job openings across industries. Searching and applying for jobs is made easy for job seekers. Indeed also provides company reviews and ratings, giving users insight into the company culture and employee experiences. They also offer additional tools that are employer-friendly and can be used during the job search.

Glassdoor is known for its company reviews and ratings. It's a platform for current and former employees to share their experiences and rate their employers. Job seekers come here to learn about company cultures, salaries and benefits. It's not just about job listings but about finding a suitable workplace. Because it provides salary data, it helps users understand what they can expect to earn in a particular role at a specific company.

Beyond the conventional

In our pursuit of the perfect candidate, we realised the limitations of traditional job-listing platforms. While they certainly have their merits, we needed a more targeted approach. Our new strategy involved identifying platforms where individuals with the specific skills we sought were already hanging out. This led us from generic job boards to more niche communities and associations. It also led us to Facebook and an opportunity to post more creative content about the company.

We tapped into platforms such as ProBrewer, Brewbound and craft beer associations. These specialised communities served as hubs for industry professionals, creating an environment where our job listings reached individuals with a passion for the craft. These sites offered both free and paid or sponsored options depending on the reach you wanted to achieve.

Our exploration did not stop at these industry-specific platforms. We ventured further: the Pink Boots Society, the Institute of Brewing & Distilling, Beer Institute and educational platforms like Blue Ridge Community College and Ab-tec, where the Craft Beer Institute of the Southeast is located. They not only exposed us to a broader talent pool but also provided unique insights into the industry landscape.

The discovery process

What we discovered was that many of these associations had their own internal job boards, creating another avenue for connection that hadn't been on our radar.

We became more creative, producing videos to showcase our company, eye-catching graphics and enhanced job descriptions that communicated our company's unusual character and requirements. We were able to share these assets on sites like Facebook to increase our presence across multiple platforms that were specific to the talent we were looking for. Eventually, we found and successfully hired some talented individuals.

The personality of the platform

During this process, the idea of platform personalities emerged. It's a concept that goes beyond the functional aspects of job sites and refers to their unique characteristics, culture and users. Understanding the personality of a platform involves paying attention to the types of people it attracts, the level of engagement within its community and the values it promotes.

By understanding the personality of a platform, you can tailor your outreach so it resonates more deeply with the audience. Whether a platform is known for its innovation, professionalism or creativity, aligning the recruitment messaging can attract top talent that fits your organisational culture. Consider bringing in your marketing team to help with this.

Once you have honed your voice, you can then participate more authentically in discussions, forums or events on the platform. This increased engagement not only showcases your company's genuine interest in the industry but also positions you as an attractive employer within the platform's community. It enables you to go beyond the transactional nature of most job listings with a thoughtful, strategic and culturally aligned approach to talent acquisition.

Who knew that the platforms you choose to showcase your job openings are the silent architects of your success? It's not about casting a wide net but about strategically crafting and placing your job adverts where the right people are hanging out.

Crafting connections

Exploring different platforms exposed us to a variety of candidates as each platform attracted its own set of unique individuals. This diversity required us to adapt our recruitment tools and techniques, ultimately leading to more successful engagements.

So, three questions to ask when choosing a platform for your job listing:

1. **Is the platform aligned with your industry?**
   Ensure that the platform caters to your specific industry or niche, giving you access to individuals with the relevant skills and expertise.

2. **Does the platform offer a community aspect?**
   Look for platforms that promote a sense of community. Communities often provide a more engaged and passionate pool of candidates who are deeply invested in the industry.

3. **What tools and features does the platform offer?**
Assess the platform's features and tools. For example, does it allow multimedia content like videos or interactive engagement? Choose a platform that can support how you want to showcase your company at its best. Sites like Indeed offer assessments that allow you to dig deeper into the recruitment process before your first contact with a candidate.

Over time, our platform strategy began to look a little different. Why not create a list of traditional and non-traditional platforms for your own industry? Working with associations, schools and organisations directly related to your industry can be the ace in the hole. At a time when traditional methods may not yield the desired results, tapping into a wider pool of candidates can be invaluable. To get you started, here are a list of non-traditional platforms that I have used:

— *DiversityJobs:* Specialises in promoting diversity and inclusion in the workplace, covering various industries.

— *Veterans Exchange:* Connects employers with military veterans seeking civilian job opportunities. Visit: *vetexchangescareers.org*

— *Health eCareers:* Targets healthcare professionals, including positions for diverse medical specialties.

— *Women for Hire:* Focuses on career opportunities for women across various industries.

— *TechCareers:* An IT job board catering to diverse candidates in the technology sector.

— *National Society of Black Engineers (NSBE) Job Board:* Specifically for black professionals in engineering and related fields.

— *iHispano:* A job board connecting Hispanic and bilingual professionals with opportunities in various industries.

— *Honest Jobs:* Specialises in connecting employers with justice-impacted candidates.

— *Disability Job Exchange:* Specialises in connecting employers with qualified candidates with disabilities. For the UK, try: *disabilityjob.co.uk*

— *Asian-Jobs:* A platform dedicated to job opportunities for professionals of Asian descent across industries. For the UK, try: *asianjobsite.co.uk*

— *American Association of People with Disabilities (AAPD) Career Center:* Focused on providing job opportunities for individuals with disabilities.

4
The numbers and the 7 P's framework

Metrics and Milestones may sound like a rock band, but they are both essential when it comes to measuring your progress. And they each serve a different purpose.

Metrics are quantitative measurements that provide data and insights about your recruitment process and the effectiveness of your strategy. For example, this could be the number of job applications you receive, the number of interviews you conduct, or the time it's taken to fill open roles. Milestones, conversely, signify the completion of a specific stage of the recruitment process, such as the candidate screening process or the first round of interviews.

Both metrics and milestones play pivotal roles in adopting a data-driven approach. This in turn informs how you recruit in the future, as it provides invaluable insight. I understand that numbers and data can sometimes be intimidating, but I've also learned that to gain the support of our superiors and foster enthusiasm among the team, our recruitment strategies must be grounded in evidence, and this can only be achieved through data.

To streamline this process and enhance its efficiency, I've developed the 7 P's framework — a simple yet potent tool to help monitor metrics, measure milestones, identify markers and, most importantly, inform and inspire your team.

So, let me introduce you to the 7 P's:

**Purpose, People, Profile, Platforms,
Process, Payouts, Pivots.**

Individually and collectively, they will help you to:

— Determine your primary intent and assemble the internal team that will support your efforts (especially if you are part of a larger organisation).

— Build a profile of the individuals you wish to recruit.

— Identify the platforms and any partnerships needed, especially if you are targeting niche markets for specific roles within the company.

— Monitor progress, allocate a budget and recognise any warning signs that may signal a change in direction is needed.

Together this data will provide you with the means to gauge the success and effectiveness of your recruitment strategy at various stages. Some of this data you can measure in fairly indisputable terms (quantifiable), while others will involve you using your judgement (qualitative).

Let's dive into each of the 7 P's.

1. Purpose

By tracking and measuring the alignment between your hires and the company's purpose and mission, you ensure that your strategy remains on track and new hires are fully on board with what the company is doing and where it's heading.

How:
Measure the percentage of hires that fully align with your company mission (quantifiable) by conducting surveys or interviews with new hires to ensure they understand the alignment between their role and the company's wider mission (qualitative).

2. People

Recruitment is a collaborative effort involving various members of the team or company. Assessing the effectiveness of your team's involvement, engagement and collaboration ensures that the 'people aspect' functions cohesively and efficiently. Metrics in this category enable you to evaluate the participation.

How:
Calculate team engagement by tracking their participation in recruitment activities (quantifiable) and gathering feedback from team members on their experience and perceived effectiveness in contributing to the recruitment process (qualitative).

3. Profile

In recruitment, you're targeting individuals with specific attributes and aspirations. Metrics associated with 'profile' help you to understand if your campaign is resonating with the right audience and attracting the candidates you want. You can then adapt your approach if necessary.

How:
Monitor the percentage of candidates who match the ideal attributes (quantifiable) and collect candidate feedback to understand if the messaging and approach resonated with their expectations and career goals (qualitative).

4. Platforms

As we heard in the previous chapter, recruitment often involves multiple platforms (or partnerships) such as job boards, social media, company websites, community-based organisations and recruitment agencies. It's crucial to measure their effectiveness so that you can allocate resources efficiently and maximise the return on investment (ROI).

How:
Calculate the ROI for each platform or partnership by comparing the amount spent to the number of successful hires (quantifiable). Monitor where applicants came from or, if unclear, ask them where they saw the job advert and which platforms they tend to use (qualitative).

5. Process

The recruitment process is the backbone of your campaign. Measuring its efficiency and effectiveness is essential. Metrics like 'time to fill', 'cost per hire' and 'candidate satisfaction' help assess and improve the recruitment process.

How:
Measure the time-to-fill metric to assess your recruitment process efficiency (quantifiable) and conduct candidate satisfaction surveys to gain insights into their experience of the recruitment process (qualitative).

6. Payouts

Recruitment campaigns can be costly, so it's vital to measure these financial aspects. This includes tracking the price of recruitment advertising, any agency fees, staff costs, platform costs to increase reach and any other expenses. This will help you manage your budget effectively and maximise your investment.

How:
Calculate the total cost per hire, including advertising, agency fees, team salaries, etc. (quantifiable). Then assess the overall impact of costs on its success, considering if the budget was well managed (qualitative). Finally, look for ways to reduce costs. For example, can you reuse elements in future campaigns?

7. Pivots

Recognising and tracking warning signs is critical when it comes to adjusting or adapting your strategy for current or future initiatives. These metrics will help you to recognise any issues at an early stage and make informed decisions to avoid costly mistakes or time-sensitive setbacks in your recruitment campaign.

How:
Track the number of significant changes or adjustments that were made for whatever reason during the campaign (quantifiable). Document and analyse the reasons behind these changes and evaluate their impact on the campaign's overall success (qualitative).

In the ever-evolving landscape of talent acquisition, mastering the 7 P's framework is not just a strategy, it's a necessity. Metrics and measurements associated with Purpose, People, Profile, Platforms, Process, Payouts and Pivots form the bedrock of this approach to build a compelling case for senior teams to justify outgoings and steer future campaigns.

By leveraging these metrics, HR professionals gain more than just numbers, they gain strategic insights. In an era where data reigns supreme, these metrics act as beacons, guiding professionals toward evidence-based decisions and helping them to spend resources effectively. They ensure that recruitment strategies align with company objectives and financial capabilities. And having these metrics to hand means you can also make a case for spending your budget on alternative approaches when those traditional routes aren't working.

For example, there was a time when people were hesitant to apply for jobs at the brewery due to past incidents associated with the company, so we needed to present the brand in a more positive light. I collaborated with the marketing team, leveraged niche platforms and hosted hiring events. During this process, managing our budget was critical. While these approaches may not apply to standard organisations, they became invaluable at TRU Colors. The alignment of our purpose with the recruitment of individuals who wholeheartedly embraced our mission, vision and values became paramount.

This is precisely why profiles matter. Some candidates came through referrals. Others came to us after learning about our mission through videos of our brewery tours posted to online job platforms.

It was a challenging time but, on reflection, these difficulties became a catalyst for uncovering solutions and creating the 7 P's framework. Experiences like this have taught me throughout my life that lived experience can become a hopeful learning experience.

5
The interview

All right, buckle up for some excitement. You've got a bunch of rock-star candidates and now it's time to meet and interview them. Prepare to channel your inner Sherlock Holmes. Discover the hidden gems among these talented candidates and decide whether they are going to be part of your dream team.

In this chapter, I'm going to help you with your interviews. I've included some 'back-pocket scripts' and you will find a Word Bank in the Resources section at the back of the book. These tools will enable you to better engage with and evaluate a candidate's responses — as it can reveal how they would likely conduct themselves should they get the job. It will also help you identify soft skills like active listening, confidence and empathy, skills that rarely appear on the resume but are desperately needed in our workplaces of today.

Be prepared

Being prepared will help you to ask relevant questions and make sure that you get all the information you need from each candidate. Before the interview, review their cv and, if you feel it's necessary, look at their online profile and conduct any further research to help you to tailor questions to their skills and experience. This may also highlight potential red flags, such as their location, that you may wish to discuss early in the process.

Set the tone

The tone of an interview should be professional yet friendly. It's important to remember that this is a two-way street and both parties should feel comfortable throughout the interview. Start by introducing yourself and welcoming them into your office space, even if the interview is being conducted online. This may seem like a small gesture, but it can go a long way towards creating a positive atmosphere and making the candidate feel at ease.

Ask direct questions

Ask questions that relate directly to their experience or qualifications, such as, 'Tell me more about your experience with X technology,' or, 'What was your biggest success in Y role?' They allow the candidate to provide insight into who they are as a professional and avoid giving yes/no answers. Additionally, ask questions that focus on their problem-solving skills.

You want to get a sense of their skill set, their level of experience—both lived and learned—and their personality to make an informed decision on whether they are suited to the role and the company.

Over the years, I've learned from speaking with HR colleagues that we often share the same nerves as our potential hires. Much like a first date, we want to make a good impression and we're eager to find that perfect match. The aim is to provide an outstanding experience that not only leaves the candidate excited to join, but also inclined to recommend your company to others. Remember, it's not just about you choosing them; they are also choosing you.

So in turn, your responses must remain professional yet friendly so that candidates feel comfortable enough to open up during the conversation, without being intimidated by your presence. While they answer each question, listen carefully, take notes and ask follow-up questions if needed.

It's also important to dress appropriately for each interview and come prepared with information and materials so the candidate feels the interview is being conducted in an organised and professional manner.

Back-pocket scripts

Here are some interview scripts to keep in your back pocket for when you discuss key areas:

Company culture

'At our company, we value collaboration and community. Can you share a past experience where you worked closely with a team to achieve a common goal? What was the outcome, and how do you think that experience might align with our collaborative culture?'

This question invites the candidate to share an experience that aligns with the company culture, fostering a connection between their experiences and the company's ethos.

Career growth

'We believe in personal and professional growth here. Can you tell me when you took the initiative to learn a new skill or take on a challenging project? How did it impact your career, and how do you see yourself continuing to grow with us?'

This question demonstrates the company's commitment to employee development and will reveal how important continued learning is to the candidate as they reflect on steps taken and their own growth potential.

Impact

'Our work often has real impact on our clients and communities. Could you share an example of a project or task where you felt you made a significant difference? How does that align with your desire to make an impact here?'

This question brings attention to the meaningful impact the company's work has. It prompts the candidate to share an example of their past contributions and align those experiences with a desire to make an impact in this new role.

Inclusivity

'Diversity, Equity and Inclusion are highly valued at our company. Can you share an experience where you actively promoted DE&I in the workplace? How do you envision contributing to our commitment to inclusivity?'

The question invites the candidate to share any contributions to DE&I initiatives that will foster a sense of alignment with the company's own commitment to these values.

Collaboration

'Our projects often require teamwork. When have you collaborated with colleagues from different departments or backgrounds to achieve a shared goal? How did your own work contribute to the project's success, and how do you see yourself operating in a similar environment here?'

This question showcases the importance of teamwork and cross-functional cooperation within the company and invites the candidate to share their experience in a previous role.

Language

It's important to maintain a respectful and positive tone in conversations and ensure that an individual's strengths and qualities are emphasised, rather than their weaknesses. This can be achieved by using asset-based language. Using the right words and the correct language matters because:

— It helps us communicate effectively

— It builds trust and rapport

— It respects cultural differences

— It promotes inclusivity and diversity

— It empowers and boosts confidence

— It aids in conflict resolution

— It enhances relationships

— It shapes branding and reputation

— It ensures legal and ethical compliance

— It attracts top talent and creates positive experiences in recruitment

Language can build a bridge or create a barrier. How we verbally interact and engage with potential team members sets the stage for the next steps. The discerning language strategy from Chapter 2 is vital here. Anyone recruiting or responsible for finding talent wants the candidate to understand what they're getting into, so use the right words to paint a clear picture. And here's the thing: language sets the tone. It's like a friendly handshake that instantly builds rapport. We want everyone, regardless of their background, to feel welcomed and valued.

Part two
Retention

6
The onboard

Welcome aboard! You've just hired a new team member
— now what? Excitement aside, figuring out how to
help them settle in can be challenging. But fear not,
I've got some simple tips to make the transition easier.
The key to their success and loyalty is a solid onboarding
process. However, before we get to that, I'd like to share
a story.

From the block to the boardroom

In most companies, onboarding is often seen as a mere
formality — introducing new joiners to their team and
giving them the basics before they go off to their
workstations. However, for TRU Colors, onboarding
became the cornerstone of the company's success.

Our onboarding wasn't just about paperwork or policies
— it was about people. We introduced newcomers not
only to the company but also to each other and, often, to
themselves. This had a transformative effect on both the
new recruits and those involved in the process. It became
a journey of self-discovery and mutual understanding that
saw strangers become teammates, friends and, in some

instances, housemates! It was incredible to witness former gang rivals become allies, and skills honed on the streets find a place in the organisation.

The onboarding process is designed to help new joiners understand their role, contribution and impact. It can accelerate belonging and build a sense of community, as well as lay the foundation for continuous learning. At TRU Colors our 'onboarding' went beyond the first few weeks — we marked achievements and milestones, celebrating the growth of both individuals and the collective team over time. Onboarding, in essence, became the catalyst for building a strong, connected and motivated workforce. Oh, and every person that we onboarded got to do a skydive at the end, too.

Over the years, I've onboarded countless individuals and found that having a simple structure in place will set the stage for long-term success.

What is onboarding?

Onboarding is organisational socialisation. It's about equipping new employees with the skills, knowledge and behaviours they need to hit the ground running and become valuable players on the team. Think of it as their official induction into the company. And guess what? It starts the moment they say 'Yes' to the job. A well-put-together onboarding process unlocks ways to help new team members get on board and, importantly, stay on board.

So, let's start with a checklist. Keep in mind that these are general guidelines that you can adapt to suit your own company, its culture and the role the person has been hired for.

The checklist

Before day one:

— Prepare a welcome package with essential documents, company goodies and a detailed schedule (see overleaf).

— Ensure all pre-employment paperwork is ready.

— If it's an in-house role, set up the employee's workspace with all necessary equipment to make them feel at home from day one. If they are working remotely, ensure they have what they need to get started.

On day one:

— Welcome the new employee with a friendly smile and introduce them to colleagues and key stakeholders.

— Ensure they have read the company's email etiquette.

— Conduct an engaging orientation session covering company policies and values.

— Give them a tour of the office or virtually walk them through if they are remote working.

During month one:

— The hiring manager should set clear performance expectations and goals to guide them towards success.

— Schedule regular feedback sessions to support their growth and development.

— Discuss professional development opportunities to enhance their career journey.

Ongoing (because onboarding is a continuous process):

— Include the new employee in team-building activities to strengthen camaraderie and collaboration.

— Invite them to company events and meetings to cultivate a sense of belonging.

— Provide continuous support and resources to ensure they have what they need.

— Follow up regularly to ensure their onboarding journey remains smooth and enjoyable.

Use this checklist as a guide to help shape your company onboarding, adding components that make more sense to your situation and removing those that are not aligned.

Friendly resources

Enhance your employees' onboarding experience right from the beginning with some supporting materials. Offer comprehensive resources such as user-friendly employee manuals, handy 'what to do when no one is around to ask or tell you' cheat sheets, and a fun and informative employee handbook — this can be print or digital. Make it exciting and vibrant by incorporating pictures of the team, past events and relevant visuals for each section.

Now, let's get into the detail of the first day and month on the team with our checkpoints and check-ins. This is a critical time. By setting expectations, offering valuable resources and promoting open communication, you will create a strong foundation for their successful integration into the company.

The checkpoints

Establish expectations early by providing a clear job description and setting some attainable goals. It is vital that everyone is on the same page right from the start. So, ensure their manager and immediate team are aware of these expectations so they can provide support when needed. It's also important that they welcome the newcomer from day one. So, make sure everyone knows who this new person is, what their role is going to be within the company and how they can best support them in their transition.

When a new person is introduced to the team in a clear and welcoming manner, it sets the tone for a positive first experience. And this doesn't always have to be in person. One of the easiest methods is a simple email introduction. It has the advantage of reaching everyone simultaneously, especially if some people work remotely, are based in another office or are simply absent that day.

It's a good idea to provide a few key details about the new joiner. Include their name, role and a brief overview of their expertise and experiences. I like to attach a picture (check the image you'd like to use with them first) to make it more personable. But why stop there? Why not sprinkle in something a little more personal or unexpected that you learned about them during the recruitment process, like the breed of dog they have or their notorious BBQ skills? This not only adds personality to the introduction but also gives the team some conversation starters. Oh, and remember to invite everyone to extend a warm welcome.

You can also use your regular internal communication platforms like Slack or Workplace as a more practical option. These platforms make it easy for team members to interact and start building their new working relationship.

The check-ins

An effective way to improve your onboarding process is to collect feedback from new employees during regular check-ins. You or their hiring/reporting manager can address any pain points and ensure their experience is smooth. It also encourages open communication from the start and creates a culture of feedback. Not only does this make employees feel seen and heard, but it also helps them understand their role and contributions within the wider company. Initially these should be weekly but can be moved to a monthly check-in to assess progress and see if additional support or guidance is needed.

Weekly check-ins

These one-on-one meetings allow open and honest discussions. They can be brief but will provide an opportunity for the hiring/reporting manager to give performance feedback, address challenges and offer any support or guidance. Use these check-ins to keep employees focused and aligned with the team's objectives by reviewing their progress on goals and projects. Encourage them to share observations and any suggestions for improvement. Make it a two-way conversation where both parties can provide feedback, and remember to actively listen. Do take this opportunity to acknowledge and appreciate hard work and accomplishments. This recognition will boost morale and motivation.

Monthly team check-ins

These check-ins can involve the wider team. It's an opportunity to share insights and best practices and for employees to learn from each other. The check-ins can be in the form of a team-building activity or a more casual meeting or hang-out. Food or snacks also help! Essentially you are creating space to discuss progress or challenges, while building relationships and creating a positive and supportive work environment. If anyone on the team is struggling or facing challenges, coming together is a great way to talk about possible solutions.

Additional feedback options

Anonymous surveys: This is a good way to get honest feedback without employees being fearful of any consequences. Periodically send out anonymous surveys so team members can voice their opinions on company matters. You can do this at no cost with a Google form which has an anonymous option where just the response is captured, and not the email address of the responder.

Open-door policy: Some managers and leaders are always there to listen. If this is you, it's a good idea to set office hours. This approach tells your team that at the specific time you list, you are open and available to discuss concerns, ideas or feedback. This policy can work in an in-office or hybrid environment and can be in-person or via video call.

Creating a culture of feedback takes commitment and effort from everyone. By fostering open communication, actively listening and taking action, you can build a more engaged and high-performing team. It's the secret ingredient that begins with the onboarding process but doesn't end there.

Beyond the block experience

At the end of the formal onboarding process, I like to do something that creates a memorable experience for new joiners. As I mentioned at the beginning of the chapter, we concluded our onboarding process at TRU Colors by taking the new recruit skydiving. It was carefully planned and budgeted, and became something the entire team looked forward to. But it doesn't have to be that extreme —it could be a coffee or a team dinner, or even something community-driven that aligns with your company mission.

And remote employees shouldn't miss out. You can ship an 'experience kit' to close out this part of the onboarding. It could be a cake-baking class or a tasting experience, for example. It's just a thoughtful way to say, 'We're paying attention and we're investing in you.'

By incorporating all of these elements into your onboarding process, you will create a positive and impactful experience that leaves a lasting impression on your new employees. Remember, we onboard to keep them on board.

Why onboarding is a must

1. **Supercharges learning and adaptation:** Give your team access to well-structured resources and manuals so they can quickly grasp processes, tools and procedures. No more slow starts. They'll hit the ground running and adapt to their roles like the pros they are.

2. **Boosts confidence and competence:** When your team receives clear instructions and knows where to find the information they need, they feel more confident.

Their competence shines through, leading to better results all around.

3. **Ensures consistency:** Company manuals and resources mean everyone follows the same practices and protocols. No more mix-ups or confusion. Your team will be a well-oiled machine, working cohesively and efficiently. Who doesn't love that?

4. **Encourages independence:** Armed with resources and clear instructions, your new joiners can work independently without constantly relying on supervisors or more experienced colleagues. They'll own their work and make confident decisions.

5. **Builds a supportive culture:** Monthly check-ins with the whole team create a supportive culture, boost morale and open communication channels.

6. **Amps up productivity and efficiency:** When you've embedded a culture of feedback and your team has easy access to the right resources, workflows become streamlined and productivity soars.

7. **Encourages knowledge sharing:** As new challenges arise and problems are encountered, making sure that knowledge is shared and resources are updated benefits everyone.

7
Retention resolutions

Let's start with a moment of reflection. Ask yourself, what steps have you taken to retain talent in your organisation? Is staff turnover increasing and, if so, can you identify the reasons behind it?

Retention is just as important as recruitment. We often put considerable energy and resources into recruitment yet fail to have a robust strategy when it comes to keeping employees once they've joined our ranks. It's essential that newly acquired employees remain invested in their work and motivated by the company's mission.

We'll learn in this chapter that retention tactics are not limited to making new hires feel welcome during their first few days. It runs much deeper. These tactics will help to instil a sense of belonging, where every team member feels they have the right to be there.

Retention is as much about creating a positive work environment, a culture of belonging with diversity of talent and thought, as it is about providing opportunities for growth and development — and, of course, offering competitive salaries and benefits. It's also about having an open dialogue with employees to understand and address their needs proactively. People are more likely to stay in a workplace that makes positivity and employee wellbeing a priority. Employees who are content and motivated are less inclined to seek opportunities elsewhere. We all know that high turnover rates can be costly and disruptive to an organisation. So for all sorts of reasons, staff retention is a vital goal.

Creating a positive environment

A positive work environment is not a matter of chance but is deliberately shaped with intention and insights gained from existing employees. When we feel valued, respected and engaged at work, we are more likely to enjoy our roles and find fulfilment. Job satisfaction, in turn, leads to higher morale and a greater sense of purpose. And who doesn't love operating from a place of purpose and being paid to do it?

Vision and leadership

It's not just about words, it's about actions. Leadership must be demonstrated through consistent communication, inclusive behaviours and leading by example. These tangible actions can be highlighted in employee newsletters, town halls or all-hands meetings. Bias-free recruitment techniques can be celebrated by sharing success stories of employees hired through inclusive processes. Show you mean business by not just implementing these strategies but celebrating them.

Equitable opportunities

Champion equitable opportunities and ensure that every
employee has a fair chance, taking into account their
backgrounds and recognising that individuals do not all
start from the same place.

Creating an inclusive environment

A culture of belonging embraces not only diverse talents
but also a myriad of perspectives. Using it as a retention
strategy involves your company taking several key steps.
Let's begin by looking at the terminology.

Belonging

Belonging is when you identify a space and place for you
without feeling othered, ostracised, overlooked or like an
outcast. It means being valued, respected and embraced
for your unique qualities, background and contributions.
In the workplace a strong sense of belonging exists where
your employees feel comfortable expressing their ideas,
collaborating with others and being their authentic selves.

Diversity

Diversity is when you can see a representation of individuals
with a wide range of backgrounds, experiences, beliefs and
characteristics in a given setting. It includes differences
such as race, ethnicity, gender, age, physical abilities,
religion, education and culture. In the workplace, diversity
acknowledges and appreciates these differences, aiming to
create an inclusive environment that values and leverages

the unique perspectives and talents of every individual. Embracing diversity fosters innovation, creativity and a broader range of ideas and approaches within the company.

Diversity of thought

Diversity of thought is when you have different perspectives and ideas offering a wide range of viewpoints, beliefs and experiences. It encourages various ways of thinking and problem-solving. Our diversity of thought is shaped by our lived and learned experiences. It has nothing to do with colour, it's partly to do with culture as it's connected to upbringing, and it has everything to do with thought processes — typically shaped by situations and circumstances that we've had to face, fix or fight through. It recognises that individuals may perceive situations differently based on their experiences, backgrounds and values. Embracing diversity of thought encourages open-mindedness, critical thinking and constructive debate. It allows organisations to consider other ideas and solutions that lead to better decision-making and problem-solving. Cultivating diversity of thought ensures that multiple viewpoints are valued and integrated into a company's strategies and initiatives.

Avoid any form of discrimination, bias or exclusion in the workplace. Failing to address any issues that may arise can undermine your commitment to diversity and inclusion. Remember that failing to speak about a problem could translate as being complicit in the issue. This area is a leading cause for why some individuals leave the workplace. Not money, not career growth, but exclusion. Yet so many organisations remain unaware of issues and problems until it's too late. Please take a moment to ask yourself: why would you stay in a workplace that doesn't accept you for who you are?

Consider running an anonymous survey to establish how employees are feeling and uncover any underlying issues. You can then formulate strategies for improvement. Your resulting data might look like this:

Belonging	52% say they feel like they belong 48% say they do not	60% agree that creating a diverse Employee Resource Group (ERG) promoting inclusivity would help bridge the gap and build connection with peers
Culture	72% feel a disconnect between the company's stated values and their actions 28% say they do feel a connection	75% say a Values Accountability Programme would help reinforce company culture

It's important to feel valued and respected in the workplace. People are realising that life is too short to spend it in an environment that makes them feel uncomfortable, undervalued or unwelcome. It's important to understand that respecting someone's beliefs doesn't mean you have to agree with them. It's about acknowledging their perspective and being open to different points of view. Creating a positive and inclusive environment requires showing respect to everyone, making them feel valued and heard.

People are increasingly seeking workplaces that align with their personal values and where they feel accepted.

During the Great Resignation, employees began to prioritise themselves and their values. Businesses that champion a culture of inclusion, respect for diverse perspectives and a sense of belonging will be far, far better equipped to retain their talent. Employee retention goes far beyond monetary compensation.

In Chapter 1, we talked about 'whole person' recruitment. This means recognising that employees bring their complete selves to work with a wealth of experiences and perspectives. To fully embrace this approach, it's crucial for workplaces to not only value diversity of thought but also create an environment where every employee feels accepted and respected for their uniqueness. As a retention strategy, this is one of the most essential for any business operating in today's dynamic and diverse landscape.

The Give Strategy

Here's how employee retention can work in practice using my 'Give' strategy:

Give a seat

Based on the make-up of your company, identify key positions, teams or regular meetings where diverse voices and perspectives are needed. This could be in leadership roles, on certain projects, or on strategic steering committees. Once you have people in place, allow them to have a voice and influence in the discussions and decision-making processes. Just remember that your next big idea could be locked inside someone with a different perspective to you that you have yet to have a conversation with.

Give a say

Establish channels for employees to communicate their opinions and ideas. These channels could include a basic communication board with sticky notes, suggestion boxes for anonymous ideas, or a 'Think Tank Thursday' where individuals gather to freely share their ideas. Or you could use more structured feedback sessions, employee surveys and the implementation of open-door policies.

The 'give a say' concept entails involving employees in decision-making processes that impact their work or the company as a whole. Encourage them to actively participate in discussions, provide feedback and offer insights. In turn, this will give them a stronger sense of belonging and ownership.

For a more structured approach, consider forming an Employee Advisory Group. This can be made up of employees from different departments and levels. The group can discuss specific issues such as workplace policies, diversity and inclusion, or improving processes. It serves as a powerful means to amplify their voices.

Give a stage

Provide a platform for employees to showcase their skills and talents, whether through presentations, workshops or knowledge-sharing sessions. This is an often-overlooked way to see hidden talents and areas of expertise within the team that may not be obvious in their daily duties.

Give a shout

Recognition and rewards are hugely significant. Celebrating individuals for their accomplishments, contributions and the varied skills they bring to the business sends a powerful message: *'We value you.'* This approach places a strong emphasis on celebrating individuality and recognising the positive impact each employee has.

It's crucial to include everyone in the distribution of acknowledgement and rewards. Often, it's the mid- and senior-level executives who are publicly honoured and celebrated at company events or all-hands meetings. To truly shape a culture of belonging and advocate for diversity, it's essential to extend this celebration from the top line to the front line.

When employees feel appreciated and acknowledged, it significantly enhances their job satisfaction and motivation. They become more invested in the company's success because they see themselves as an integral part of it. And ultimately, they are more likely to stay at a place where their contributions are valued.

Give a path

Establish a career development path for all employees, with a strong emphasis on equal access to these growth opportunities and promotions. Professional growth and development are essential when it comes to retention. Providing staff with the tools and opportunities they need to continue learning is vital. A successful Professional Growth and Development (PG&D) programme should empower employees with career advancement opportunities in-house, increase job satisfaction and align the growth of the individual with the growth of the company. It will foster loyalty, reduce staff turnover and maintain a skilled and committed workforce.

Create structured career development plans for each employee, regardless of their level. These plans outline clear steps, milestones and expectations for career progression. Provide resources and support for employees to reach these milestones, including training and mentorship. Regular reviews and updates to these plans will ensure they align with both individual aspirations and the needs of the company.

By offering a tangible roadmap for employees to advance in their careers, your company is demonstrating that they are invested in the growth and success of every employee, irrespective of their background or perspective. It shows that diversity and inclusivity are not just buzzwords being thrown around but integral to the daily operations of the business and the future trajectory of the people who work there.

You might like to turn career development into a gamified experience. This was something I implemented as part of a larger strategy to not only retain, reward and recognise employees but also build community. Employees were encouraged to navigate their career path like a game. They could earn points, badges or rewards for completing training modules, reaching milestones or taking on new responsibilities. This not only made the career development process more engaging but also encouraged employees to actively chart their progress and seek out growth opportunities.

When it comes to promotions, it's important to implement an equitable and fair process. Ensure that promotions are based on merit, skills and contributions rather than biased judgements. Use objective criteria and clear performance evaluations in decision-making. Try and make the promotion process as transparent as possible and provide feedback to employees who are not selected, offering guidance on areas for improvement and future opportunities.

Establish an internal jobs marketplace where staff can explore open projects, temporary roles or job rotations within the company. Create a platform where they can express interest in or apply for these opportunities.

This initiative is a great way for employees to explore different career paths and expand their skill sets without leaving the company. And it fosters a culture of continuous learning and adaptability.

What can we achieve together?

The beauty of the Give strategy lies in its shift from the traditional mindset of *'What can the organisation do for me?'* to a more forward-thinking approach of *'What can we achieve together?'* Moving from the individual to the collective, it can be applied to drive meaningful change and growth within the wider organisation.

This paradigm shift redefines the relationship between employees and employer to one of collaboration, inclusivity and collective growth. It's a departure from the more self-focused approach to career development and workplace dynamics. It encourages employees to see themselves as active participants in the journey of the whole company, rather than passive beneficiaries of its offerings. They are empowered to contribute their unique skills, talents and ideas for the greater good of the business, their colleagues and themselves.

The Give strategy can be expanded to a series of innovative approaches that go beyond traditional HR practices, such as:

— **Give a hand:** Implement mentorship programmes that pair experienced employees with newcomers, fostering professional growth and inclusivity.

— **Give a chance:** Provide opportunities for employees to lead or contribute to diversity and inclusion initiatives, cultivating a sense of purpose and empowerment.

— **Give a nudge:** Encourage employees to seek out new opportunities that foster personal and professional growth. It may require them to step out of their comfort zones and explore new experiences, which can be the key to unlocking growth.

— **Give a handshake:** Promote networking and relationship-building among employees, creating connections among those with different backgrounds and perspectives.

— **Give a listening ear:** Create a culture where active listening is valued. Enable employees to share their concerns and ideas without fear of reprisal. Refer back to Chapter 6 where we talked about check-ins and feedback.

— **Give a vision:** Communicate a vision to the entire company, outlining the importance and benefits of culture, community and conversation.

— **Give a story:** Share the success stories of employees, highlighting their journeys and achievements within the company to inspire and motivate others.

— **Give a commitment:** Commit to continuous improvement by regularly assessing and enhancing initiatives based on feedback and data.

These Give strategies can be adapted to your company's specific needs and goals, ultimately contributing to its culture while boosting employee retention and satisfaction.

The listening strategy

Even though all of these topics are an important part of ensuring that your employees stay put, how we communicate has proven time and again to be critical when it comes to staff retention.

Open lines of communication are the cornerstone of any retention strategy. When your team can express themselves and engage in meaningful dialogue with their peers, supervisors and management, it creates an environment that values the importance of communication.

Let's start with how you hear. Listening is a principal component. It involves not only hearing what is being said but also understanding the underlying emotions, concerns and unspoken messages. It goes beyond just acknowledging words, it's about genuinely understanding the speaker's perspective. And it's a critical workplace skill for both leaders and colleagues.

Active listening

This goes beyond merely waiting for your turn to speak. It's about tuning in so your employees feel fully heard. When you're in conversation, convey a sincere interest in what the speaker is saying and allow them the space to express themselves without fearing judgement. An excellent way to exhibit active listening is through direct eye contact. While it might initially feel somewhat uncomfortable, nothing conveys *'I'm here and I'm listening'* better than a focused gaze. Furthermore, be mindful of your posture. Folded arms could signal defensiveness and impatiently tapping fingers imply that you have somewhere else to be.

Global listening

This is next-level listening that goes beyond verbal communication to encompass non-verbal cues from the person you are listening to. These subtle signs can range from a raised eyebrow to a hesitant tone, often conveying unspoken concerns and emotions. Being more attuned to these non-verbal signals displays a deeper level of empathy and understanding.

When we listen, we want to try and hear not only what our employees are saying, but also what they are expressing without words. Often, just before people decide to leave their job, they may stop communicating. In a previous company, we used the Slack app for much of our everyday communication. Occasionally I would notice someone being far less active on the channel and, if this continued for two weeks or more, I might regard them as being at risk — exploring other job opportunities or holding in something that needed to be addressed.

Other non-verbal clues

Pay attention to what employees communicate in writing too. This includes emails, feedback sessions and ideas shared during meetings. You won't always need to act on this information, but it can sometimes give you clues if an employee isn't happy or is feeling unmotivated.

The same goes for their actions and behaviours. What projects do they choose to work on? How do they interact with colleagues and clients? How do they react in various situations? Again, their non-verbal communication can provide insight into areas where they might need support or development or reveal interests which can be harnessed and might encourage them to feel more connected with the workplace. You may find that certain topics or issues evoke strong emotions among employees. Understanding what stirs them up, whether positively or negatively, can help you get a sense of their core values and what's important to them. This can present opportunities for engagement and alignment.

Compensation and benefits

In the world of talent retention, you'll never get away from competitive pay and good benefits. Money isn't everything, but it matters when you want to attract and keep hold of the best employees. While you may not be able to influence the salary and pension plan offered, perhaps you can develop an attractive 'smart benefits' package. Regardless of the shape and size of your business, you can offer unique perks that suit people at different stages of their lives and careers. It's time to reimagine how you retain.

Firstly, let me introduce my Lifestyle Concierge service. Okay, maybe it's not as grand as it sounds! During the onboarding phase, invite new employees to fill out a simple questionnaire to better identify current and longer-term needs or interests. They can then be presented with a list of available company benefits that are tailored to them, for example, gym memberships or subsidised travel.

People spend so much time working that company benefits or incentives can be a real perk. Some of these might include:

— Stock options, equity, profit-sharing

— Housing and transportation programmes

— Tuition reimbursement

— Paid time off, paid parental leave, family planning and sick pay

— Childcare assistance

— Wellness programmes (see *mental health support*)

— Bereavement (see *grief support solutions*)

— Discounts at local and national brands (see *partnerships*)

— Employee assistance

— Mentorship programmes

Mental health support

Global events like the pandemic and the accompanying distressing news bulletins have taught businesses to pay closer attention to how external factors impact the mental health of their team. In terms of company benefits, consider offering access to mental health support, whether through online therapy services, in-person consultations or apps like BetterHelp, Thrive, Calm and Headspace. And for physical health and wellbeing, you can offer discounted gym memberships, massages or acupuncture. Some schemes don't have to cost anything. Why not encourage staff to set up their own walking or running club? This not only promotes health and wellbeing but also builds community.

Beyond that, consider hosting workshops that focus on mental health and wellbeing. On one occasion, we organised a health fair and brought in mental health specialists, created a quiet room for reflection, hosted art therapy sessions and connected employees with a range of professionals in the mental health field. It's about taking care of the whole person.

Grief support solutions

Bereavement is one of those really important components that we need to do more to rally behind. It's not intentionally ignored among all of the other 'stuff' centred around people strategy or benefits, but it's like the elephant in the room. No one wants to talk about the thing we most fear, but we have to.

I didn't understand the depth of the need for better bereavement policies until I started losing people in my life. It really hit home hard when I lost my mom, and I needed all the support I could get. I took her to the ER for a muscle sprain that she had been getting treated for the past 6 months, and it turned out that it was cancer that had spread to her ribs and other areas of her body. My heart broke, but I was ready to fight. The fight never came. After waiting for results, the doctors said mom was too weak for chemo, and there was nothing they could do. I moved into the hospital room with her and was back and forth at work, which was a few blocks from the hospital, for a month. I needed that time.

The day she passed away, I didn't know what to do. My world stopped. I was both in pain and in panic but had to be strong. Everyone, especially my younger sisters, leaned on me for support.

Bereavement policies are usually 3–5 days for immediate family members and shorter for extended family members. But how on earth could I come into work after losing the woman who brought me into the world after just a few days and be on my A game? I consider myself incredibly strong and resilient, but I cried in the company's bathroom, during lunch breaks in my car and in between meetings.

I needed more time and space but also needed to be able to financially support the household. The company

I worked for at the time extended the bereavement leave that I needed — something that I hope you will consider in rewriting your policies around what to do when an employee loses a loved one. Here are some strategies you might consider, using the acronym 'Grace':

G — Grief support: Offering grief counselling services or support groups for employees dealing with loss.

R — Rest and recovery: Extending the duration of bereavement leave beyond the standard 3–5 days, especially for the loss of immediate family members. Bereavement Leave Policy Enhancement acknowledges that grief doesn't have a set timeline.

A — Assistance: Offering financial support or assistance, especially if the deceased was a primary provider. At TRU Colors we partnered with a local hospice that provided information around counselling and end of life planning. Employees could also opt in to a funeral fund, contributing $10 or more from each pay cheque.

C — Compassionate communication: Ensuring open, empathetic and ongoing communication with bereaved employees. Encouraging managers or teams to commemorate the deceased loved one in a respectful and supportive manner, such as sending a card or flowers, or attending services, if appropriate.

E — Empathy in policy: Creating policies that genuinely reflect understanding and compassion for the grieving process. These might include flexible return-to-work options, bereavement training for managers and access to mental health resources, including grief counsellors or employee assistance programmes.

Bereavement is a critical aspect of employee wellbeing that requires thoughtful and compassionate handling. These strategies can help in making the workplace a more supportive environment for those experiencing loss.

Professional development

As we saw with 'give a path', a compelling incentive to both join and stay is the opportunity for professional development. People want to know that they will continue to learn and develop new skills after they have joined the company. If budget allows, offering a professional development stipend is a great way to support this journey.

Regular training sessions, workshops and educational offerings encourage employees to enhance their skills and knowledge. This can be facilitated through a dedicated Professional Development Fund, access to online educational platforms like Udemy, edX or Coursera and other relevant resources.

You can also offer mentorship programmes that connect experienced employees with newer team members. These programmes facilitate knowledge transfer, professional growth and a sense of belonging. Once you pair people, you can use a feedback survey to measure the impact that the mentorship has on the individuals concerned and the company as a whole.

You can also have a speaker programme. At TRU Colors we ran regular 'Lunch and Learns' to bring the staff together and gain knowledge. Experts from the local community came in to give a short talk over lunch (or after work). It never ceased to amaze me how many were keen to share their knowledge or services, and most of them would turn down the offer of a fee. Speakers ranged from finance experts advising on home buying or budgeting tips to health and wellbeing professionals, local authors and motivational speakers. If you have a number of remote workers, you could record and share these sessions internally, but do always ask the permission of the speaker.

These extra-curricular activities have the added benefit of forging connections and sparking meaningful conversations among employees.

Partnerships

Lastly, consider partnering with local and national stores to offer discount codes to staff. If they need persuading, you could perhaps suggest a reciprocal arrangement where you offer something in return — discounted goods or services, for example, that you produce in-house. These can be great incentives and most can be added without any upfront cost.

An effective retention strategy is like a well-tailored suit — it needs to fit your company culture, your budget and the diverse needs of your team. And remember, it's an ongoing journey. You will need to constantly assess what's working and what isn't. Make adjustments, adapt and review. What you are trying to do is create a positive and supportive environment where your entire team feels valued and motivated and wants to stay. Lastly, it goes without saying that it is essential to ensure that all the benefits and opportunities within the business are accessible to all team members.

8
The stay interview

If someone submits their resignation, it's essential to take their reasons seriously and explore ways to address any issues. I'm always so invested in the people I hire that if they want to leave, it's like a breakup I didn't see coming! Emotions aside, you'll want to take action quickly to try to retain them, and that's what this chapter is all about.

First of all, invite them to come in for a 'Stay Interview', rather than moving straight to an exit interview. Traditionally, exit interviews consist of need-to-know dates tied to last pay cheques, benefits and the handover of job duties. Let's change it around. If the employee you are speaking to is someone who has been extremely valuable to the company and their leaving would create strain, it's well worth conducting a stay interview in the first instance.

This conversation can provide insights into their reasons for leaving and give you the opportunity to come up with some steps you might take to retain them. It's also when I deploy the KIND code, an acronym for 'Knowledge Inspires New Direction'. I'll explain more later in the chapter, but you can use any insight and data obtained during the stay interview to define and design a retention or 'stay strategy'. This will help keep your star performers in place and, hopefully, deter others from leaving.

I like using the KIND acronym. In today's workplace, kindness has evolved into a multifaceted concept that encompasses both emotional warmth and tangible actions aimed at helping others or oneself. While kindness has always been important, its role in organisational settings has become a strategic approach. Kindness is not synonymous with passivity. Instead, it's about being active — active listening, inclusivity, understanding.

Questions you ask during the stay interview may reveal why the employee is leaving, what would or could make them stay and/or what the business could have done better. It also serves as an intervention — a responsive approach to address the resignation in the hope of finding a solution or strategy that genuinely resonates with the employee, encouraging them to reconsider. And if they insist on leaving, at least they will hopefully do so with a positive perception of the company.

I understand that this situation can be awkward, because most individuals who have submitted their resignation have typically either secured another opportunity or reached a breaking point after a period of prolonged dissatisfaction. Even if their physical presence remains, they've often mentally checked out. However, if we are focused on whole person recruitment and the creation of a positive work environment, it's imperative that we invest in one final effort to engage with and support the individual in question.

Preparation is key

To adequately prepare for the stay interview, it's a good idea to invest some time in getting to know the person in question a little better. I would hope that you know all your employees already, but that is not always the case. Having a clear understanding of the job role they are resigning from, the significant contributions they've made during their tenure and the specific projects they've been involved in will help tailor the conversation to highlight their unique impact on the company. It will allow you to make the stay interview more personal and meaningful.

You should also focus on understanding their journey: when they started, the importance of their role and what they've accomplished. When employees feel that their contributions and journeys are acknowledged and valued, it builds trust. Trust is essential in convincing them to reconsider their decision to resign and stay with the company.

This effort demonstrates that they are not just a statistic as they depart. Such personal interaction helps build the relationship we will discuss later, where employees leave with a sense that they are known and understood. This understanding is what drives that valuable connection.

During the interview

Take notes: It's essential to record the key points discussed during the interview for future reference, especially in developing other retention strategies. This includes constructive feedback and practical insights provided by the individual. This data could become a critical resource for your company.

Uncover icebergs: The stay interview is a valuable opportunity to identify hidden issues within the company. Often, there may be underlying concerns or challenges that have been lingering unnoticed. By addressing these concerns either immediately or in the future, you can prevent them from becoming larger problems.

Examine influence: Try and establish whether they have shared any issues with other team members. Understanding whether they've discussed their departure and with how many people can provide insights into the morale of the wider team. Has the person shared information about their new job (if they have one), or have they communicated how they feel about leaving? This knowledge can be crucial for managing the impact on the team and providing support to ensure a positive and respectful departure experience for employees while minimising disruptions to the company.

Stay positive and respectful

When the stay interview begins, take a moment to express gratitude. Show genuine appreciation for their contributions and dedication to the company throughout their time with you. Specifically, acknowledge any notable efforts and achievements, providing validation that goes beyond routine acknowledgement. This personal validation not only fulfils them on an emotional level but also plays a role in maintaining a positive relationship. Satisfied former employees will speak positively about their experiences and create a powerful word-of-mouth effect that might attract new talent. It also leaves the door open for any future opportunities, fostering a positive and lasting connection.

When employees feel genuinely valued and acknowledged, they are more inclined to offer honest feedback during the interview. This is invaluable for the ongoing growth and improvement of the company. So, treat the person respectfully and recognise their accomplishments.

Now, you've arrived at a pivotal juncture in your conversation. You believe in the value of the relationship between you and your employee, and it's at this moment that you present your proposition. It might sound unconventional, but keep in mind the words of renowned rapper and street philosopher, Eminem: 'You only get one shot.' This is your chance to convey your sincere interest in them staying with you.

In this conversation, you're not offering financial incentives — at least not initially. You're extending an opportunity to continue the relationship, taking into account the insights and feedback garnered during your preparation. If the discussion goes well, it signifies a commitment from you to their ongoing development within the company. If you begin by offering money, this can be a flawed strategy, as it conveys the message that values and loyalty can simply be bought. The Great Resignation has taught us differently.

To enhance your effectiveness in convincing employees to stay before they resign, consider implementing some of the retention strategies outlined in Chapter 7. However, if, despite your efforts, they still decide to leave or you know that they need to go, it's important to part ways professionally. Sometimes, a fresh start benefits both the employee and the company.

This is the point where you transition to discussing the next steps in a respectful and supportive manner. Your stay interview will then lead into a farewell conversation or what is more traditionally known as an exit interview.

Discussing final pay and benefits, and the return of company items where applicable, can be tricky. To make the process smoother, use a transition sheet. This covers vital information about the final pay cheque, benefits, compensation and anything else the employee is owed before they leave. There is a sample transition sheet on pages 102–3.

The KIND code

During this process the KIND code gives you a framework to obtain the information you need to make intentional impact. It will also help keep you grounded, ensuring that decisions are made with empathy and respect. This approach contributes to the more humanised, home-grown and responsible human resources experience we've been speaking about throughout this book, where the wellbeing of both the employee and the company is at the forefront. The chart opposite explains the application of the KIND code.

At the end of the stay interview, collect and analyse the KIND data about why the employee is leaving to identify trends and concerns. Incorporate these insights into ongoing HR practices and use them to help shape your retention strategies, ensuring a continuous cycle of improvement based on real-time data.

Knowledge

Question

What do you know about the individual and why they are leaving?

Implementation

During the conversation, ask open-ended questions to encourage the individual to share their experiences and reasons for leaving. Actively listen to understand their perspective.

Activation

Acknowledge their 'why' while creating a non-judgemental atmosphere so they feel comfortable sharing their perspective. Use any insights to address their specific concerns, tailoring your approach to advocate for them to stay based on their unique situation.

Inspires

Question

How has this inspired you to advocate for them to stay?

Implementation

Recognise patterns in their positive experiences and identify what motivated and inspired them so that you can shape that into ideas.

Activation

Share insights about how their continued presence aligns with their personal and professional growth. Use their sources of inspiration to rekindle their enthusiasm and create a compelling case for them to stay.

New Direction

Question

How can you move forward with this information?

Implementation

Use the information gathered to suggest alternative paths within the company.

Activation

Discuss potential opportunities, fresh challenges and career development options that align with their aspirations.

Transition sheet for departing employee

[Your Company Name]

Employee information

FULL NAME:

EMPLOYEE DEPT:

DEPARTURE DATE:

Responsibilities transition
— List of ongoing projects and their current status.
— Key responsibilities and tasks to be handed over.
— Name and contact information for employees taking over tasks.
— Any unfinished work or pending deadlines.

Knowledge transfer
— List of critical knowledge areas for the role.
— Contacts or resources for further information.
— Documentation, manuals or processes.
— Training materials or access to relevant systems.

Company property
— Inventory of company-owned equipment or assets in the employee's possession.
— Instructions for returning company property.
— Deadline for returning property (if applicable).

Final pay and benefits
— Details about the final pay cheque, including the payment date and how it will be allocated.
— Information about accrued holiday or leave days.
— Benefits continuation, if applicable.
— Instructions for handling retirement accounts or other financial matters.

Additional information
— Stay interview details and schedule (if applicable).
— Contact information for HR or relevant departments.
— Any other relevant information for a smooth transition.

Employee's acknowledgement
I, [employee's full name], acknowledge that I have received and reviewed this transition sheet. I understand my responsibilities regarding the transition process and will adhere to the provided instructions.

SIGNATURE:

DATE:

Supervisor's acknowledgement
I, [supervisor's full name], acknowledge that I have discussed the transition process with the departing employee and provided the necessary guidance.

SIGNATURE:

DATE:

This sample document can be amended to fit your company's specific needs.

9
Let go with LOVE

I've been laid off in the past and without question it's one of life's most challenging experiences. The feeling of letting down not only the company, but also yourself, can be overwhelming and hurtful. The idea that your contributions no longer align with the needs of the company is heart-wrenching. And even being let go due to financial constraints does the same. I've experienced that too, and even witnessed the abrupt closure of TRU Colors.

This chapter looks at letting go with love and why it's essential to have this as a guiding principle. We'll discuss the emotional and financial impact, as well as the legal considerations to take into account. And I'll give you some back-pocket scripts to pull out when you need to have the hard conversations so you can extend the help that you can, and provide the hope that you should.

The three types of letting go

There are three distinct types of workforce departures. The first involves being laid off because of budget constraints that make it impossible to sustain the entire team.

The second relates to termination resulting from performance issues. And the third relates to being fired for a direct violation of company policies and procedures. Regardless of the specific category, it's undeniable that strong emotions are always attached.

Whatever the reason, the idea of 'letting go with love' doesn't change — even though some may think it should. What remains constant is the internal culture guiding your actions. An individual may have erred, but you stay committed to doing what's right. You want to approach the complicated process of saying goodbye with a compassion that reflects the company values and preserves the dignity of the individual.

Letting people go is a challenging process that involves someone's wellbeing and livelihood. Often, we are unaware of an individual's emotional, mental and financial state when it's time to let them go. However, what we do know is that these layoffs occur for valid reasons.

In both my experiences of being let go, there was a distinct lack of empathy. The reasons for letting me go weren't for any significant wrongdoing, although that didn't make it any easier. The first was down to a difference in opinions, and the second was purely an economic decision. In the first case, I chose to stick to my principles rather than stay for the pay cheque.

Both were a long time ago now, but that first time I was asked to leave the building after years of service. My belongings were packed up, except for my personal Rolodex, which the company saw as valuable — they even disposed of pictures that held sentimental value to me. I cried for days and lost all confidence. It took a long time to get that back.

The second time, I was informed that the pay cheque I was due to receive in 48 hours would be my last. This meant that my livelihood, which I used to pay bills and share expenses with my husband to support our home and children, was suddenly gone. The company wouldn't know this but, to make matters much worse, the very next day my father was hospitalised after a routine doctor's appointment. He passed away a week later.

Laying off employees with empathy and compassion matters. Why? Because it can significantly reduce the emotional and financial stress experienced during such a difficult time.

We need to remember that behind every job, there's a person with their own unique circumstances and struggles. Assuming that employees will be fine and neglecting to show any care for their feelings and emotions, despite any established workplace norms, reflects a self-centred perspective. Part of the intent of this book is to turn that perspective upside-down.

Now, I understand that the mention of 'love' in the context of employment terminations may seem unusual but it's also a word that signifies the caring and compassionate approach that companies should adopt. You're trying to make a challenging process more humane. Harvard Business Review recently highlighted the business case for love in the workplace, signalling a change in perception.

By being transparent and providing resources and support, communicating regularly, treating employees with respect, offering a fair severance package if possible and even helping them plan for the future, you can help them make it through with minimal disruption.

Legal considerations

When it comes to addressing the legal aspects of terminating employees, it's a complex landscape due to the differentiation in laws, not only between countries but also within individual states or regions.

To mitigate legal risks and ensure compliance, you need to have a consistent standard operating procedure (SOP) in place that aligns with your state or country's employment laws. This SOP should outline the steps and procedures to be followed when terminating an employee. I would recommend working closely with legal experts who have expertise in employment law specific to where you are based and considering best practices in HR management.

This procedure is critical for the company and its employees. It will help to strengthen trust and alleviate anxiety for those involved.

The LOVE framework

It's important to be transparent and honest with your employees about the reasons for layoffs, the impact on the company and the timeline for the process.

1. Let go with LOVE due to financial constraints

Here are some key considerations to keep in mind if you need to let people go due to budget constraints:

L — Listen and learn: Take time to understand the individuals who will be affected. Listen to their concerns, learn about their specific circumstances and empathise with their situations. Provide a safe space for employees to share their thoughts and feelings. Listen actively and ensure they feel heard and respected.

O — Offer support and resources: Prepare a comprehensive support package, including access to career counselling, resume writing services, job placement assistance and mental health support. Share these resources with those affected, ensuring they know where to turn for help.

V — Value their contributions: Acknowledge and appreciate the work of those impacted. Highlight their achievements and the value they have brought to the company. Express gratitude for their past contributions. Make it clear that the decision is about the company's financial position, not a reflection of their worth.

E — Empathise and explain: Put yourself in their shoes. Consider how the news will impact them and their families. Prepare clear and compassionate explanations about why this is happening. Share the reasons by explaining the business context and what led to this difficult decision.

When TRU Colors closed, we had mental health professionals who dedicated 90 days to providing emotional and mental health support to team members. We contacted our local community college, asking them to send experts in cover-letter writing and resumes to help employees update these vital documents. When you've been working for an extended period, creating a fresh and compelling resume can be overwhelming, and these experts were invaluable.

We also leveraged additional resources, including partnerships with companies who were actively hiring. This might sound unconventional but, again, it's a reflection of my belief in creating a more human-centred approach — one that shapes our systems, processes and policies to revolve around supporting people during good times, bad times and uncertain times.

I even reached out to other businesses (that weren't facing the same challenges as us) and invited them to join us for what I called a 'pink slip party'. It had never been done before but at these gatherings, our teams would meet potential employers face-to-face, exchange handshakes and have conversations. The result was that several people secured employment with these participating organisations, and many of them still work there to this day.

While these 'parties' weren't a celebration, they were innovative and viable solutions to support employees during this time. It demonstrated that even when faced with the difficult decision to let people go, we were still committed to investing time, energy and resources into those people we had worked with, and who had worked with us.

2. Let go with LOVE due to performance

What if you find yourself in a situation where you have to consider laying people off because they're consistently not reaching their goals?

This is a difficult place to be. Whether we choose to admit it or not, firing someone who's not meeting their goals or for some other reason relating to their performance is one of the hardest things that we have to do. More often than not, these individuals are not inherently bad employees; they may well enjoy their roles and get on well with colleagues. However, despite best intentions, they consistently fall short of meeting goals and deadlines.

Of course, before taking the dismissal route, there are a few important steps to consider. Have you provided or attempted to implement a professional development or performance improvement plan to help them get back on track and learn how to meet their targets? It's essential to offer a tool that could support them. This signifies a commitment to their growth and success. But if you've already taken these steps and clarified that the performance improvement plan will lead to dismissal if the necessary changes are not achieved, then you can apply the same LOVE framework to this situation. Here's how:

L — Lead with empathy: Begin the conversation with empathy, acknowledging the challenges they've faced in meeting their goals. Express your understanding of their efforts and struggles.

O — Open communication: Maintain open and honest communication throughout the process. Share the reasons behind the potential dismissal and the impact.

V — Valuable resources and support: Offer resources to help them find new opportunities or undergo further professional development. This doesn't have to be done on a case-by-case basis. It could be a community resource guide suitable for everyone. Encourage them to seek career counselling and resume writing services. You can include an information sheet about this in the paperwork.

E — Ensure fairness: Implement the process fairly, adhering to company policies and treating all employees consistently and equitably.

When applying the LOVE framework in this context, you can navigate the difficult task of potentially dismissing employees who haven't met their goals with empathy and respect. This approach ensures that, even in challenging moments, the company values its employees' wellbeing and seeks to support them in their career journeys.

3. Let go with LOVE due to misconduct

Now comes the most challenging scenario: how do you uphold the principles of 'love' as outlined previously, when you're required to terminate someone for a rule violation, policy breach or misconduct? This individual may have committed an offence that fundamentally contradicts what the company represents. They might have taken a short-cut in a process, manipulated the system or engaged in inappropriate behaviour.

Maintaining your commitment to a more humanised, equitable and compassionate approach when dealing with someone whose actions contradict your core values and standards is a test. Let's be honest, it's like having to hold your tongue when you know that if you respond in the wrong manner, it will reflect poorly on you, even though you're not in the wrong!

So, you should still aim to approach this situation with love, as if it were either of the previous two categories. In this instance, it requires practice and resilience. It's undeniably difficult, as these situations often involve subjective judgements. Your own biases or past experiences might be triggered, making it crucial to view each case through the lens of equity. The principles must be universal, not contingent on the specifics of who, what, when, where or why.

Here's how you can apply the LOVE framework in the context of this challenging scenario:

L — Lead with empathy: Begin the conversation with empathy, understanding the gravity of the situation. Express concern for their wellbeing and future prospects.

O — Open communication: Maintain open and honest communication during the process. Clearly convey the reasons for their termination and the impact on the company.

V — Valuable resources and support: Offer information about resources that can help them during their transition, such as job search assistance or access to employee assistance programmes. Encourage them to seek counselling or support services, especially if the dismissal is a result of their own actions.

E — Ensure fairness: Implement the termination process fairly, following company policy and treating the individual consistently and equitably.

Again, this approach underlines your commitment to upholding company values. It's about handling a difficult situation with compassion and fairness.

LOVE yourself

As you negotiate these difficult conversations across three different categories, it's equally vital to learn how to apply the LOVE framework to yourself. As a founder, HR professional or workplace warrior, you've encountered many scenarios throughout this book, addressing recruitment, retention and responsibility. Now, it's time to extend that same compassion and understanding to yourself. This approach not only nurtures your own wellbeing and professional growth in the field of human resources, but also benefits your team members.

The LOVE framework for founders, HR professionals, managers and all other workplace warriors:

L — Lead with self-compassion: Begin by showing yourself the same empathy you extend to others. Acknowledge that you, too, are human, and it's okay to make mistakes or face challenges.

O — Open reflection and learning: Maintain open communication with yourself, nurturing a growth mindset. I don't mean talk to yourself, I mean listen to yourself. Are you exhausted? Are you working towards a goal and facing challenges? It's important that, as leaders, we learn to communicate with ourselves and respond effectively in the same way we communicate with others. Reflect on your experiences, both positive and negative, to identify areas for personal and professional development.

V — Valuable self-care and support: Prioritise self-care and ensure you have the physical and mental resources to fulfil your role effectively. Seek support and resources for your own wellbeing, including mentorship, coaching or counselling when needed.

E — Ensure fairness: Hold yourself to the same standards of fairness and equity you uphold for others. Avoid biases and remain consistent in your decisions and actions while upholding company values. Perform quarterly self-checks.

Back-pocket scripts

As promised, here are some 'back-pocket scripts' for laying people off with LOVE in the categories we discussed. The suggested wording is designed to convey empathy, respect and support while addressing the various scenarios with care and compassion.

Due to financial constraints:

Introductory statement:
'Thank you for joining me today. I understand that this is a challenging time, and I appreciate your dedication to our

LET GO WITH LOVE

company. Unfortunately, we're facing financial constraints that require us to make some tough decisions.'

Offer support:
'We want to support you through this transition. We can help connect you with potential employers, training opportunities and financial advisors. We're also here to assist you with any immediate needs you may have, such as completing necessary paperwork or addressing your concerns.'

Due to performance:

Introductory statement:
'First and foremost, I want to express our appreciation for your hard work and dedication to your role. We understand that, despite your best efforts, you've been facing challenges in meeting your targets and goals.'

Offer support:
'We're committed to helping you through this transition. We've arranged a personalised career counselling session for you and access to performance improvement plans. Our aim is to support your growth and provide resources that can help you navigate your next career step.'

Due to misconduct:

Introductory statement:
'I want to acknowledge the situation at hand that has led us to having this difficult conversation. We value the contributions you've made to the company. Unfortunately, there have been violations of company policies and procedures.'

Offer support:

'We're here to assist you during this transition. We've partnered with mental health professionals who are available to provide emotional and mental health support if you need someone to talk to. We also have resources to help you with your career transition if that's the path you choose.'

10 tips for having difficult conversations

When it comes to dismissing someone, the conversation can be extremely challenging. I've put together a few tips and techniques to help you conduct it more effectively.

1. **Prepare and plan:** Before the conversation, take time to prepare and plan what you want to say. Outline the key points you need to address and consider the potential responses.

2. **Choose the right time and place:** Find a quiet, private space where you won't be interrupted and a time when both parties can focus without distractions.

3. **Active listening:** Let the other person express themselves fully before responding. Use non-verbal cues such as nodding to show you're engaged.

4. **Stay calm and on topic:** Maintain your composure and complete focus on the issue at hand. Avoid getting sidetracked by unrelated issues or emotions.

5. **Use 'I' statements:** Frame your concerns using 'I' statements to express your feelings and perspective without blaming or accusing the other person.

For example, *'You're always late'* could become
*'I understand you have a difficult commute, however,
we can't keep delaying the team meeting...'*

6. **Ask open-ended questions:** This style will encourage
a productive dialogue and typically invite the other
person to share more. For example, *'Can you tell me
more about how you see this situation?'*

7. **Avoid making assumptions:** Don't assume you
know the other person's thoughts or intentions.
Instead, ask for clarification and seek to understand
their perspective.

8. **Offer support and options:** Where possible, provide
support and suggest potential solutions. Offer choices
and empower the other person to make decisions.

9. **Set clear expectations:** Clearly communicate what
you expect moving forward and any changes that
should occur. Make sure that both parties involved
have a mutual understanding of the next steps.

10. **Follow up:** After the conversation, follow up to check
on progress and show your commitment to resolving
the issue. This reinforces that the conversation was
more than just a one-off event.

The LOVE framework keeps us connected and allows us
to uplift one another even in challenging times. It's a
practical and proven approach that can provide hope and
possibilities for all.

10
That's a wrap

Recruitment and retention are often seen as industry buzzwords but I hope that you now share my belief that they represent the foundation of our businesses and the people who fuel them. More than just a process, they are invitations and promises to those people we bring in. And, just as crucially, they are strategies for keeping them.

In a world where the dynamics of work continue to shift, we have the opportunity to drive change within our businesses and our lives. Every time one of us takes a step to transform how we do things, we become a beacon, an example for others to follow. Our actions today shape the future of work and influence the lives of those we touch.

Hiring the right people is just the beginning. As we've seen, it is equally important to create a positive work environment that encourages employee engagement, fosters collaboration and supports career growth because we want employees to stay. When you focus on retention as much as recruitment, you demonstrate that you value your employees and the contribution they make to the company.

In these chapters, we've gone deep into recruitment as a holistic experience, emphasising the importance of whole person hiring. We've learned that creating an inclusive, empowering workplace culture is vital in attracting the right people and ensuring they want to stay.

When I discovered that there was a void in our practices, I took the initiative to create new solutions. And when existing systems weren't effective, I rebuilt them from the ground up. It's easy to get caught up in the comfort of maintaining the status quo, avoiding making waves or causing disruptions. However, in doing so, we may unknowingly disrupt our own growth and potential, and that of our company.

For the longest time, I was hesitant to stand out, to be different or pioneer change. But I've come to understand that someone has to take that first step. My hope is that *Do Recruit* is a testament to the power of embracing change, switching up our strategies and leading from the heart in the world of work.

The approaches I've shared will not only enhance employee wellbeing but also boost morale, leading to higher levels of job satisfaction and increased productivity. In addition, when you can effectively apply these behaviours to your organisational blueprint, it results in a positive return on investment that benefits the bottom line.

As we bring *Do Recruit* to a close, let's return to the whimsical wisdom of Dr. Seuss, a master at uncovering the extraordinary within the ordinary. His stories inspire us to embrace the full spectrum of possibilities, urging us to say yes wholeheartedly to potential and innovation. In a world as ever-changing as the fantastical landscapes of Seuss's imagination, we too can be the architects of change. Adopting his approach of kindness, creativity and inclusivity, we can transform our HR practices into a more personalised, humane experience. When employees feel seen, heard, valued and supported, they engage more deeply and are motivated to contribute their best.

Kindness and empathy encourage inclusivity and respect, and cultivate a workplace where people genuinely want to come to work.

Remember, you are perfectly equipped for this journey. *'Oh, the places you'll go!'*

Good luck, I'm rooting for you!

Appendix: Strategies for when the going gets tough

In challenging times, when numbers don't align, the workforce might seem scarce and world events or a difficult boss create problems within the company, it's crucial to be resilient, adapt to changing circumstances and keep your focus on the bigger picture. Here's a recap of key areas we've discussed to help you when things are tough.

1. **Reconnect with your purpose:** Start your journey by reminding yourself of your 'why'. Why did you choose a career in recruitment or a closely connected field like HR? Embrace your passion for connecting people with opportunities and making a positive impact.

2. **Set clear intentions:** Set specific goals and intentions for your recruitment efforts. Having a clear focus will keep you motivated and help you measure your progress.

3. **Leverage your network:** In times of workforce shortages and external crises, the power of your network can be a game-changer. Reach out to your professional connections for insights, referrals and support. Sometimes, the ideal candidate is just a connection away.

4. **Revamp your job descriptions:** Refresh your job descriptions to make them more appealing and engaging. Show candidates why your opportunities are exciting.

5. **Sharpen your interview skills:** Enhance your interview techniques to ensure you're selecting the best candidates. Practise active listening and probing questions.

6. **Innovate your sourcing strategy:** Explore new platforms and methods for sourcing talent. Be open to unconventional channels and technologies. Review your platform analysis or make this the perfect time to begin one. What has worked, what hasn't and what's next?

7. **Cultivate empathy:** Develop empathy for candidates' needs and aspirations. Understanding their perspective can help build stronger connections. Lay off in LOVE, activate the KIND code and prioritise the whole person, not just their skills and experience. Empathy builds connections that transcend professional boundaries.

8. **Foster belonging and a DE&I workforce:** Prioritise diversity, equity, inclusion and access in your recruitment efforts. Celebrate different backgrounds and experiences.

9. **Embrace technology:** Leverage AI, automation and data analytics for more data-driven recruitment. Stay up to date with the latest tech solutions and trends.

10. **Personalise your approach:** Tailor your communication and engagement with candidates. A personalised touch can go a long way.

11. **Seek feedback:** Encourage candidates to provide feedback on their experiences of your recruitment process and onboarding. Use their insights to improve.

12. **Show gratitude:** Express gratitude to your candidates and colleagues. A simple 'thank you' can go a long way in building positive relationships.

13. **Upskill:** Commit to lifelong learning. Stay informed about industry trends, best practices, current and new ways of working.

14. **Narrate:** Learn to tell compelling stories about your company and the opportunities you have available. Stories connect with potential candidates on an emotional level.

15. **Define balance:** Remember to maintain a work-life balance to avoid burnout. Take care of your own wellbeing. Practise mindfulness to stay present and focused. It can help reduce stress and improve decision-making.

16. **Boost your online brand:** Enhance your online presence. Share your expertise and insights through blogs or social media.

17. **Cultivate patience:** Patience is crucial in recruitment. Keep calm and trust the process.

18. **Learn from mistakes:** Acknowledge your mistakes and use them as learning opportunities for growth.

19. **Adapt and innovate:** Be open to changing your strategies when necessary. The ability to adapt and innovate is key in the ever-evolving recruitment landscape, especially when existing methods haven't yielded results. Take calculated risks, challenge traditional norms and be open to reshaping recruitment processes.

20. **Promote collaboration:** Collaborate with your team. Combined efforts can have outstanding results.

21. **Build long-term relationships:** Focus on nurturing long-term relationships with candidates and clients. Think beyond the immediate hire. I use a 2–2–2 method for making meaningful connections. Two days to check in after meeting, two weeks to schedule a virtual or in-person coffee and two months to reconnect if we haven't been in touch.

22. **Improve time management:** Master time-management skills to make your recruitment processes more efficient.

23. **Celebrate successes:** Take time to acknowledge and celebrate your successes, both big and small.

24. **Empower candidates:** Empower candidates to make informed decisions about their careers. Provide them with valuable insights and advice.

25. **Prioritise self-care and reflection:** Give yourself time to reflect on your journey and ensure self-care remains a priority. Recruit with passion, purpose and resilience.

Resources

The Word Bank

Dip into this bank of asset-based words, provided here with definitions, and use them in interviews or conversations with candidates and employees to convey their strengths and qualities, i.e. their assets rather than deficiencies:

Adaptable: Demonstrates flexibility and the ability to thrive in changing environments.

Adaptive learner: Quickly acquires new skills and knowledge to adapt to new challenges.

Collaborative: Thrives in team settings and contributes positively to group dynamics.

Courageous: Willing to take risks and tackle challenging situations head-on.

Customer-focused: Prioritises meeting the needs and expectations of customers or clients.

Dependable: Consistently delivers on commitments and responsibilities.

Detail-oriented: Has a keen eye for precision and accuracy in work.

Effective communicator: Conveys thoughts and ideas clearly and persuasively.

Efficient: Maximises productivity and minimises wasting time and resources.

Empathetic: Understands and relates to the perspectives and feelings of others.

Empowering: Encourages and supports others to reach their full potential.

Innovative: Brings fresh ideas and creative thinking to the table.

Leader: Exhibits qualities that guide and inspire others.

Motivated: Demonstrates a strong drive to achieve goals and excel.

Organised: Manages tasks, time and resources efficiently.

Positive attitude: Maintains a constructive outlook, even in challenging situations.

Proactive: Takes initiative and anticipates challenges to address them in advance.

Problem-solver: Excels at analysing issues and finding practical solutions.

Resilient: Bounces back from setbacks and remains determined in adversity.

Resourceful: Excels at finding creative solutions and maximising available resources.

Respectful: Treats others with courtesy, dignity and respect.

Results-oriented: Focuses on achieving measurable outcomes and objectives.

Shows initiative: Takes action independently to drive progress and improvement.

Strategic thinker: Can see the bigger picture and plan for the long term.

Team player: Values collaboration and contributes to the success of the team.

The following are words described as 'non-asset-based' and are ones I would recommend avoiding in interviews or conversations so that you maintain a positive and respectful tone:

Apathetic: Indicates a lack of motivation or enthusiasm.

Careless: Suggests a need for more attention to detail.

Discouraging: Implies a lack of support for others' potential.

Disorganised: Indicates a need for more order and efficiency.

Disrespectful: Suggests a lack of consideration for others' feelings.

Follower: Suggests a lack of leadership qualities or independent thinking.

Fragile: Implies vulnerability to stress or challenges.

Inflexible: Indicates resistance to change or lack of adaptability.

Insensitive: Implies a lack of empathy or understanding towards others.

Negative attitude: Indicates a pessimistic or defeatist outlook.

Obstacle: Implies a focus on problems rather than solutions.

Passive: Suggests a need for more initiative or action-taking.

Poor communicator: Suggests difficulty in conveying thoughts and ideas.

Reactive: Indicates a tendency to respond only when problems arise.

Self-centred: Suggests a focus on personal needs over others.

Shortsighted: Suggests a lack of long-term planning or vision.

Slow learner: Implies a difficulty in acquiring new skills or knowledge.

Solitary: Suggests an aversion to collaboration or teamwork.

Stagnant: Implies a lack of growth or progress.

Timid: Implies a fear of taking risks or confronting challenges.

Unproductive: Indicates a need for more focus on achieving outcomes.

Unreliable: Implies inconsistency in meeting commitments.

Unresourceful: Suggests a need for more creativity in problem-solving.

Wasteful: Indicates inefficiency in resource management.

About the author

Khalilah 'KO' Olokunola is not your ordinary HR professional. An Impact Architect and the founder of ReEngineering HR, her clients include Patagonia and many others. She is known for transforming company culture and creating innovative hiring and retention strategies aligned with a company's mission and values. Prior to founding ReHR, Khalilah served as Chief People Officer at TRU Colors, a brewery with a social mission to reduce violence in the community by employing active gang members.

Khalilah is an inspirational speaker. Her work has been featured in print, online and on TV, including *Forbes* and *Good Morning America*. It has earned her recognition as an HR innovator and Conscious Business Leader.

She is married with four children. She calls Wilmington, North Carolina, home by way of Brooklyn, New York.

khalilaholokunola.com | @khalilahequips

Thanks

Thank you's are so hard. You fear you're going to miss someone, or miss saying something you've had on the tip of your tongue that is really meaningful but you can't quite convey. I hope my heartfelt gratitude is expressed here.

First, I want to thank God. I wrote the book in the middle of many challenging moments and couldn't have made it this far without Him.

My husband Al, whose boundless love, patience and understanding have been one of my greatest sources of strength. You have been my rock throughout this journey.

To our children, Miya, Anna, Kairos and Adam, your endless love, joy and laughter have filled my life with purpose and inspiration. Thank you babies of the 'O' bunch for your understanding during those late nights and weekends spent writing.

I am deeply grateful to my Pastor Daniel Cook for his guidance and wisdom which have been a constant source of inspiration.

To my dear friend and confidante, Dr Elisa Lashell Harney, your unwavering support, encouragement and belief in my abilities have been a driving force behind many endeavours including this one. Thank you for always being there to lift me up when doubt crept in.

A special acknowledgment to Duke Stump, whose introduction opened my eyes to a world of unlearning and growth through Bonfire and then at DO. Your sharing of space has been invaluable in shaping my perspective and continued approach to life and work.

To George Taylor, the work at TRU has and continues to inspire me. Thank you for the push into the industry and the opportunity to work in an organisation where innovation, compassion and empathy became my driving forces.

Though they are no longer with us, I carry the love and support of my parents, who believed in me and supported me unconditionally. Your legacy lives on in every page of this book.

Last but not least, I extend my gratitude to the Talent Nova team and all of the HR professionals who generously shared their knowledge and expertise, allowing me to listen and learn from their experiences early on in my career.

To each of you, I am profoundly thankful for your contributions, guidance and unwavering belief in me. This book would not have been possible without your love and support.

With deepest appreciation,
KO

Books in the series

Also available

Available in print, digital and audio formats from booksellers or via our website: **thedobook.co**. To hear about events and forthcoming titles, find us on social media **@dobookco**, or subscribe to our newsletter.